Rethinking the Qur'ân:
Towards a Humanistic Hermeneutics

Rethinking the Qur'ân:

Towards a Humanistic Hermeneutics

Nasr Abû Zayd

HUMANISTICS
UNIVERSITY
PRESS

Extended version of the inaugural address of 27 May 2004 at the occasion
of the acceptance of the Ibn Rushd chair of Humanism and Islam at the
University for Humanistics.

Humanistics University Press is a SWP imprint for publications
of the University for Humanistics (Utrecht, The Netherlands)

Rethinking the Qur'ân: Towards a Humanistic Hermeneutics
Nasr Abû Zayd

ISBN 90 6665 605 0
NUR 717

Contents

Introduction

The world has already become, whether for good or for bad, one small village in which no independent closed culture, if there is any, can survive. Cultures have to negotiate, to give and take, to borrow and deliver, a phenomenon that is not new or invented in the modern context of globalization. The history of the world culture tells us that the wave of civilization was probably born somewhere around the basin of rivers, probably in black Africa, Egypt or Iraq, before it moved to Greece, then returned to the Middle East in the form of Hellenism. With the advent of Islam, a new culture emerged absorbing and reconstructing the Hellenistic as well as the Indian and Iranian cultural elements before it was handed to the Western New World via Spain and Sicily.

Shall I mention here the name of the Muslim philosopher Ibn Rushd, known as Averroes in the Latin environment and the importance of his writings in constructing synthesis of both the Aristotelian and the Islamic legacies, thus, transfusing new intellectual light to the European dark ages?

I would like to take the opportunity to express my gratitude to the Humanist Foundation 'Socrates', the Humanist Development Organization, HIVOS, and the Board of Governors of the University of Humanistics for the very significant initiative to establish an Academic Chair for Islam and Humanism in the Arabic name 'Ibn Rushd' instead of the Latin Averroes. I am so honored to be the first scholar to occupy the Chair, and in the vein of Ibn Rushd's thought I hope not only to present my lecture today, but more to contribute to the process of building solid bridges between Islam and Humanism.

Why is it now so vital for Muslims to rethink the Qur'ân? Besides the present context of Western Islamophobia, especially after the trauma of September 11th and the aftermath terrorism operations everywhere in the Muslim as well as the non-Muslim World, which reduced Islam to be radical, violent and exclusive, one should emphasize the importance of this invitation to 'rethink the Qur'ân' for Muslims in general, and for Muslims living in Europe in particular. I am not here claiming any missionary task to formulate a specific Islam, but rather situating my hermeneutical position.

The process of 'rethinking tradition' as well as negotiating the 'meaning' of the Qur'ân in the Muslim World has been, however, an ongoing development since the eighteenth century. I would like to argue not only for the continuation of this process of rethinking but for moving it further toward a constructive method for Muslims, wherever they are, to be actively engaged in formulating the 'meaning of life' in the world in which they live.

In the year 2000 I was honored with the Cleveringa rotated Chair of Law, Freedom and Responsibility, especially Freedom of Religion and Conscience by the Chair's curatorium at the University of Leiden. In my inaugural lecture on Monday 27 November 2000, exactly three and a half years ago, I presented the concept of the Qur'ân as a space of Divine and Human Communication. Under the title 'The Qur'ân: God and Man in Communication', I attempted a rereading, and therefore re-interpretation, of some basic principal assumptions contained in the classical disciplines, known as 'the sciences of the Qur'ân', `ulûm al-Qur'ân in Arabic, especially those sciences which deal with the nature of the Qur'ân, its history and its structure.

In such rereading, and re-interpretation, I employed some methodological apparatus, such as semantics, semiotics as well as historical criticism and hermeneutics that are not generally applied, nor appreciated, in the traditional Qur'ânic studies in the Muslim World. I focused in my analysis on the *Vertical* dimension of revelation, *wahy* in Arabic, i.e., the communicative process between God and the Prophet Muhammad that produced the Qur'ân. As these vertical communications, which lasted for more than 20 years, produced a multiplicity of discourses (in the form of verses, passages, short chapters) these discourses had a chronological order.

In the process of canonization, from which the canonized scripture emerged as *mushaf*, this chronological order was not preserved; it was replaced by what is now known as the 'recitation order' while the chronological is know as the 'decadence order'. According to the orthodox view, the Qur'ân was perfectly preserved in oral form from the beginning and was written down during Muhammad's lifetime or shortly thereafter when it was "collected" and arranged for the first time by his Companions. The complete consonantal text is believed to have been established during the reign of the third caliph, `Uthmân (644-56), and the final vocalized text in the early 4th/10th century. It is important, even if we uncritically adapt to the Orthodox view, to realize another human dimension present in this process of canonization, which entailed the early rearrangement and the late application of signs of vocalization to the only consonantal script.

Today, I would like to develop my thesis about the human aspect of the Qur'ân one further step, moving from the vertical dimension towards the *Horizontal* dimension of the Qur'ân. By the horizontal dimension I mean something more than the canonization, or what some other scholars identify as the act of the prophet's gradual propagation of the message of the Qur'ân after receiving it, or the spread of the message through the 'interpretive corpus', according to M. Arkoun. I do mean the *horizontal* dimension that is embedded in the structure of the Qur'ân and was manifest during the process of communication itself. This horizontal dimension could only be realized if we shift our conceptual framework from the Qur'ân as a 'text' to the Qur'ân as 'discourse'.

1- The Qur'ân as 'Discourse'

Recently, Muhammad Arkoun and others[1] rightly distinguish between the phenomenon of the Qur'ân, the recited discourse, and the *Mushaf*, which contains what Arkoun identifies as the 'Closed Corpus' or Scripture through the process of canonization explained

1   See Muhammad Arkoun, Rethinking Islam, common questions, uncommon answers, translated by Robert D. Lee, Westview Press, 1994, pp. 35-40; The Unthought in Contemporary Islamic Thought, Saqi books & the Institute of Ismaili Studies, London 2002, p. 99. See for the views of Hasan Hanafî my Naqd al-Khitâb al-Dînî (Critique of Religious Discourse), Cairo, second edition, p. 187.

above, which transformed the recited discourse into scripture or a 'text'. Today I would like to bypass this historical moment of transformation known in the history of every religion. Since that historical moment Muslim scholars of the Qur'ân, though theoretically aware of the impact of this transformation and occasionally return back to the pre-text structure of the Qur'ân, never were able to recapture the living phenomenon, the Qur'ân as a 'discourse'.

Modern scholars of the Qur'ân share the concept of the Qur'ân as a 'text' despite the different paradigm of 'meaning' each tries to grasp and deduce from the Qur'ân. Dealing with the Qur'ân as only a 'text' enhances the possibilities of interpretation and reinterpretation but allows as well the ideological manipulation not only of the meaning but also of the 'structure', following the pattern of polemic interpretation of theologians.

I was one of the propagators of the textuality of the Qur'ân under the influence of the literary approach initiated by the modern, and still appreciated, literary approach[2]. I recently started to realize how dealing with the Qurân as a text alone reduces its status and ignores the fact that it is still functioning as a 'discourse' in everyday life.[3] The volume entitled 'The Qur'ân as Text', which presents the proceedings of the symposium held in 1993 in the Oriental Seminar of the University of Bonn, enjoyed so many reprints[4], because it introduces the shift to which Stefan Wild refers, at least in the Western Qur'ânic scholarship, from the paradigm of the 'genesis' of the Qur'ân, whether Jewish or Christian, to the paradigm of *textus receptus*.

It is true that the Qur'ânic *textus receptus*, the Qur'ân as a text contained in the *mushaf*, shaped and shapes the religious convictions of Muslims and is, more the central cultural text in so many Islamic

2 See for example my Mafhûm al-Nass: drâsa fî `ulûm al-Qur'ân (The Concept of the Text: study in the Qur'ânic sciences, Beirut and Casablanca, first published 1990, fourth reprint 1998 and other later publications. For more about the literary approach see my 'The Dilemma of the Literary Approach to the Qur'an', in ALIF, Journal of Comparative Poetics, the American University Cairo (AUC), No. 23, Literature and the Sacred, 2003, pp. 8-47.

3 I owe this realization to the research for writing a long article about 'the Qur'ân in Everyday Life' to the Encyclopaedia of the Qur'ân, Brill Leiden (henceforth EQ), vol. 2 (2002), pp. 80-98.

4 Stefan Wild (ed.), E.J, Brill, Leiden, first print 1996.

cultures.[5] But this is true only when we limit our definition of 'convictions' and 'cultures' to the high level, the 'convictions', and 'cultures' of the elite. On the lower level of 'cultures' and 'convictions, on the level of the masses, it is more the recited Qur'ân, the phenomenon of the Qur'ân as discourse, that plays the most important rule in shaping the public consciousness.

For Muslim scholars the Qur'ân was always a text, from the moment of its canonization till now. It is time now to pay close attention to the Qur'ân as discourse or discourses. It is no longer sufficient to re-contextualize a passage or some passages when it is only needed to fight against literalism and fundamentalism or when it is needed to wave away certain historical practice that seems unfit in our modern context. It is also not enough to invoke modern hermeneutics in order to justify the historicity and, therefore, the relativity of every mode of understanding claiming in the meantime that our modern interpretation is the more appropriate and the more valid. These insufficient approaches produce either polemic or apologetic hermeneutics.

Without rethinking the Qur'ân, without re-invoking its living status as a 'discourse', whether in the academia or in everyday life no democratic hermeneutics can be achieved. Why it has to be democratic? Because it is about 'meaning of life' it has to be democratically open hermeneutics. If we are sincere in freeing religious thought from power manipulation, whether political, social, or religious in order to return the formulation of 'meaning' back to the community of believers, we need to construct open democratic, humanistic hermeneutics.

The empirical diversity of the religious meaning is part of our human diversity around the meaning of life in general, which is supposed to be a positive value in our modern living context. In order to re-connect the question of the meaning of the Qur'ân to the question of the meaning of life it is now imperative to indicate the fact that the Qur'ân was the outcome of dialoguing, debating, augmenting, accepting and rejecting, not only with pre-Islamic norms, practice and culture, but with its own previous assessments, presupposition, assertions etc.

5   Ibid., p. viii in the introduction.

It might be surprising to claim that - in the early Muslim era, before the Qur'ân was fully canonized, and definitely before Islam was fully institutionalized - the differentiation between the Qur'ân, the still alive discourse, and the *mushaf*, the silent text, was explicated against an invitation to politicize the Qur'ân. This moment needs to be remembered.

2- The Qur'ân versus the Mushaf: the spoken and the silent

I would like here to start with a statement related to the Fourth caliph, `Alî, the cousin of Muhammad and his son-in-law, in which he described the *mushaf* as silent; it does not speak, but humans speak it out. The context in which this statement emerged is important, because it could shed a lot of light on the present situation in which the political manipulation of the meaning of the Qur'ân is hardly cancelled.

It was in the context of `Alî, the legally chosen Caliph, fighting against Mu`âwiyya, the governor of Syria who did not recognize `Alî's authority, in the battle of Siffîn in 657. Mu`âwiya's star seemed to be sinking, when his collaborator `Amr b. al-`Âs advised him to have his soldiers hoist copies of the Qur'ân on their lances. This gesture, famous in Muslim history, did not imply surrender; by this means Mu`âwiya invited the combatants to resolve the question by consultation of the Qur'ân. Weary of fighting the two armies laid down their arms. `Alî was forced by his partisans to submit the difference to arbitration, as proposed by Mu`âwiya, and further to choose the arbitrator for his side from among the "neutrals". So sure were his followers that they were in the right! In these decisions the *qurrâ'*, those who memorize the whole Qur'ân by heart and are the professional recitors, played a large part. The mission of the arbitrators was to consult the Qur'ân "from the first to the last sûra" and, in default of clear indications in the sacred Book, the sunna of the Prophet, excluding what might give rise to divergences. In the absence of a clear definition of subject of consultation, certain individuals had protested against recourse to arbitration with the cry *lâ hukma illâ li'llâh*, literally "no arbitrator but God". The phrase implied that it was absolutely improper to apply to men for a decision since, for the case in dispute, there existed a divine ordinance in the Qur'ânic verse 49:8-9: "If two parties of the Believers fight with one another, make peace between them, but if one rebels (*baghat*) against the other, then fight against that one which rebels (*allatî tabghî*), until it returns to obedience to God ...". The dissidents maintained that it was `Alî's duty to continue to fight against Mu`âwiya, as no new fact had intervened to alter the situation. [6]

In response to such a cry `Alî made the differentiation between the silent *mushaf*, the text, in one hand, and the vocalized Qur'ân by the people on the other hand. This statement of `Alî, which is heavily quoted by modernist Muslim scholars merely to indicate the multiple possibilities of interpretation, as well as the possibility of political manipulation of the Qur'ânic meaning, has more implications than has been realized. The vocalization of the Qur'ân, whether in liturgy, in everyday life, in any social, political or ethical dispute, carries with it certain mode of interpretation and re-interpretation by ways of intonation and appropriation.[7] The Qur'ân is a living phenomenon, like the music played by the orchestra, whereas the *mushaf*, the written text, is analogous to the musical note; it is silent. A humanistic hermeneutics of the Qur'ân must take seriously the living phenomenon and stop reducing the Qur'ân to the status of *solely* a text.

The modern political Islamist movements whether radical or moderate agree on God's absolute authority in determining and stipulating the regulations of the detailed behavior of the individual as well as the laws that govern the society as a whole. In modern political hermeneutics such a claim of the absolute Divine source of legislation, is based on the similar claim of the protestors against arbitration. While the protestors of the seventh century cried 'no arbitrator but God' by interpreting the Qur'ânic vocabulary *yahkum* as to judge or arbitrate the modern political protestors understand the same word as to rule by way of legislation.

This political and ideological manipulation can also be found in the classical era of Islam. Based entirely on an explicit assertion that the Qur'ân is only a text, its manipulation continued.

---

6   Cf. article `Alî b. Abû Tâlib, the Encyclopedia of Islam, E. Brill (henceforth EI), Leiden, 2ed edition, vol. 1, p. 381ff.

7   For examples of different ways of intonations and appropriations of the Qur'ânic verses see the article 'Everyday life, Qur'ân in' EQ, vol. 11, op cited.

3- The 'Text' Reconstructed and Manipulated

When I started to examine the different methods of interpretation applied to the Qur'ân as a 'text' in traditional Islamic theology in my first book (1982),[8] I investigated the emergence of the concept of "metaphor" that was introduced to Arabic rhetoric at the beginning of the 9th century by the rationalist school of theology, known as the Mu`tazilites, through their effort to explain the anthropomorphic images of God in the Qur'ân, on the one hand, and the verses that seem to support a doctrine of "predestination", on the other. The Mu`tazilites employed the concept of "metaphor" as a linguistic tool to interpret those types of verses of the Qur'ân that they considered "ambiguous". This forged a powerful instrument to interpret the Qur'ânic text according to the Mu`tazilites' transcendentalist standards: where it suited their ideas, the Qur'ânic text was labeled "clear" and, therefore, not in need for metaphorical interpretation; where it did not, it was considered to be "ambiguous" and need to be interpreted metaphorically.

The main conclusion I have reached, after comparing the Mu`tazilites' and the anti-Mu`tazilites' discourses, was that the Qur'ân became the site of a fierce intellectual and political battle. That battle was sited at one of the most important junctures of the structure of the Qur'ânic text (Qurân, 3:7).[9] Both the Mu`tazilites and their opponents agree on the principle that the Qur'ân includes ambiguous verses as well as clear verses, and that the "clear" should furnish the norms for disambiguating the ambiguous. However, they disagree when it comes to practical implementation; thus, the con-

---

8 Al-Ittijâh al-`âqlî fi 'l-Tafsîr: Dirâsa fî Qadiyat al-Majâz fî `l-Qur'ân `nd 'l-Mu`tazila (The Rational Trend in Qurânic Exegesis: investigation of the concept of 'metaphor' in the Qur'ân established by the Mu`tazilites), The Arabic Cultural Center, Casablanca and Beirut, first published in 1982 and so many reprints followed.

9 He it is Who has sent down to thee the Book: in it are clear, well established verses; they are the backbone of the Book: others are ambiguous. Those in whose hearts is perversity follow the part thereof that is ambiguous seeking discord and searching for its hidden meanings but no one knows its hidden meanings except Allah and those who are firmly grounded in knowledge say: "We believe in the Book; the whole of it is from our Lord"; and none will grasp the Message except men of understanding. Reference to Qur'ânic citations are indicated always in this paper by the chapter's number according to Cairo edition followed by the verse or verses' number. For translation, Yusuf `Ali's is used as only guiding reference.

troversy does not only revolve around the meaning of the Qur'ân, it also involves its structure. What the Mu`tazilites consider as "clear" is considered as "ambiguous" by their opponents, and vice versa. Such intellectual disputes about the structure and the meaning of the Qur'ân constituted the first hermeneutical principle as the dichotomy between clarity and ambiguity.

The intellectual opponents of the Mu`tazilites were the traditionalists, who upheld the literal interpretation of all Qur'ânic verses, to the extent that they affirmed the existential reality of all divine attributes, all the eschatological images, and even the idea that God can be seen by human eyes. The Mu`tazilites objected to their idea that the literal interpretation of the holy text was a religious duty, regarding it as an obstacle to the fulfillment of mankind's destiny. They believed that God himself imposed on mankind the duty to acquire real knowledge by using his rational faculties.

Later I will explain that this conjecture declaring 'clarity' and 'ambiguity' in the Qur'ân is part of the dialogue discourse of the Qur'ân, the dialogue with the Christians of Arabia, the *Nasârâ*. For the theologian to assume an establishing rule or a principle of hermeneutics required the assumption of the 'textuality' of the Qur'ân.

As for the jurists, their approach is based on another structural principle that differentiates between the 'early' and the 'late' revelations. According to this principle, there should be no contradiction in any prescription or proscription, because the 'late' always abrogates the 'early'.

Though they seem to ascertain awareness concerning the Qur'ân as 'discourse', it presented them with a problem that needed to be solved. They did not understand that the different rulings of the Qur'ân could be a positive phenomenon, a diversity that should be kept open as options for the community of believers to be able to compete with the ever-changing social order; instead they aimed at fixing the meaning by considering the gradual process of revelation as gradual development in the content of the message. Considering the later revelation to be the final and the previous to be provisional they applied the concept of 'abrogation', thus, eliminating all the previous options in favor of the last revealed articulation. According to this concept of abrogation the Qur'ân is divided into four categories:

1- Verses and passages that are entirely deleted from the present Closed Corpus, i.e., they once belonged to the Qur'ân, but now they no longer belong to the Qur'ân.

2- Verses and passages whereby their rules and stipulations are no longer valid, but still exist in the Qur'ân to be recited; their legal power is deleted but not their divine status as God speech.

3- Verses and passages whereby their rules and stipulations are valid though they are deleted from the Qur'ân; the stoning penalty for fornication committed by married people belongs to this category.

4- Of course the verses and passages that were not subject to abrogation.[10]

The Sufi hermeneutics might be the possible ingredient for an open democratic hermeneutics in the Islamic culture. Muhyî 'Dîn Ibn `Arabî, the great Andalusian Sufi who was born in Spain, wrote his greatest treatise in Mecca (The Meccan revelation, *Al-Futûhât Al-Makkiyya*) and died in Syria (638/1279). His hermeneutics of the Qur'ân formed the topic of my second book (1983),[11] and planted the seeds of a possible open democratic hermeneutics. Ibn `Arabî's hermeneutical project is based entirely on emphasizing the inclusive nature of the Qur'ân, meaning bringing together, versus the *Furqân*, another name of the Qur'ân meaning the separation and differentiation.[12] By such emphasis he constituted an attempt to integrate all knowledge existing up to his time (from Plato to Averroes) in the Qur'ân; his hermeneutics opens the meaning of the Qur'ân, and the meaning of Islam, to be very conclusive meaning that integrates Christianity, Judaism, and all other religions. Ibn `Arabî's Islam is a religion of comprehensive love, as Ibn `Arabî terms it in his poetry.[13] The hermeneutics of the Sufi in general, and of Ibn `Arabî, follows it

10 For more detailed explanation see art, nashk by J. Burton in EI, vol. V11, pp.10010ff. See also the same author's article 'abrogation' in EQ, Brill Leiden vol. 1, 2001, pp. 11ff.

11 Falsafat al-Ta'wîl: dirâsa fî ta'wîl 'l-Qur'ân `in Muhiyî Dîn ibn `Arabî (The Philosphy of Hermeneutics: study of the Ibn `Arabî's Hermeneutics of the Qur'ân The Arabic Cultural Center, Casablanca and Beirut, first published in 1983 and so many reprints followed.

12 See article 'tassawuf', in EI, vol. x, pp. 317ff.

13 "My heart has become capable of every form: it is a pasture for gazelles and a convent for Christian monks, And a temple for idols and the pilgrim's Ka`ba and >

in general not in details, depending basically on the notion of four semantic levels applicable to every verse: the outward (*zâhir*), the inward (*bâtin*), the limitation (*hadd*), and the upward (*matla*). This multi-semantic structure of the Qur'ân enabled the Sufis to avoid the dichotomy of clarity and ambiguity employed by the theologians, because every level leads to the upper and contains the lower with no contradiction nor dichotomy. It also keeps the Qur'ân accessible to all the believers regardless of their education or their intellectual capacity.

Ibn Rushd critically developed the Mu'tazilite system further in order to open up the meaning of the Qur'ân to the findings of philosophy. According to him, the Qur'ân, being intended to address and reach all humans, regardless of color, ethnicity or level of knowledge, includes three modes of semantic expression. The first, and most common, is the outward poetic (*khâtabî*) form addressing the masses; the second is the argumentative (*jadalî*) form intended to address the theologians; the third and most refined is the philosophical (*burhânî*) form intended for the philosophers.[14] The difference between Ibn Rushd and the theologian, against whom he launches a severe attack accusing them of destroying the masses' convictions by propagating their interpretation as the only valid understanding, is that he does not consider the poetic meaning, addressing the masses, as inferior to the philosophical. He asserts the difference not the hierarchy. His being a jurist, a physicist as well as a philosopher might explain his unique position. Although he quotes the conjecture verse (3:7), always invoked by the theologian to reconstruct the Qur'ân in terms of 'clarity' and 'ambiguity', he only used it as a justification, alongside other legal principles - such as legal syllogisms, the right of the philosophers to be engaged in hermeneutics. Ibn Rushd' hermeneutics have not yet been studied probably because his theological treatises did not go beyond these general outlines. A thorough study of his hermeneutics would need to investigate his total writings, including his commentaries; he was after all deeply involved in a heavy interpretative task.

the tables of Torah and the book of the Koran. I follow the religion of love: whatever way Love's camels take, that is my religion and my faith." See. Ibn Al-`Arabî's Tarjumân Al-Ashwâq, a collection of mystical odes (The Interpreter of Desires), trans. By Reynold A. Nicholson, London 1911, p.67

14 Cf. On the Harmony of Religion and Philosophy, translation of Ibn Rushd's Fasl al-Maqâl by George Hourani, E. Brill, Leiden 1992, Chapter 3.

So far the Sufi hermeneutics, which emphasizes the semantic multiplicity in accordance with the recipient engagement in producing the meaning, seems closer to recognizing the nature of the Qur'ân than are the theologians, the philosophers (except Ibn Rushd perhaps), and the jurists. They were able, according to the notion of individual engagement with the Qur'ân, to develop the concept of '*samâ*'' (listening attentively) and so present the other side of the coin, the Qur'ân, meaning vocalization and recitation. Dealing with the Qur'ân as a text alone would find 'interpretation' to be the other side of the coin, in this case the *mushaf* not the Qur'ân.

Now, the question is, 'could any hermeneutics ignore the fact that the Qur'ân is not *only* a text?' So far, the history of exegesis shows that the Qur'ân has been dealt with as a text that needs only a structural and philological analysis to uncover its meaning. This is obvious in the theological as well as the philosophical approach, which is built on the assumption of the 'clarity-ambiguity' dichotomy, and which survived until today. As we have seen already such a dichotomy facilitates the semantic manipulation of the Qur'ânic meaning. Dealing with the Qur'ân as 'discourse' would present a rather different paradigm that might enhance our proposed hermeneutics.

What follows will only offer some examples of the some characteristic of the Qur'ânic discourse; a comprehensive and detailed projection needs a book. I hope that the following examples will present only the skeleton of a broader project.

4- Polyphonic not Monophonic, Who Speaks and Who Listens?

Because the concept of the Qur'ân as only 'text', predominates in both east and west there is a difficulty in presenting an accurate typology of the Qur'ânic structure The Encyclopedia of Islam's categorization of the 'Literary Form' of the Qur'ân, for example, is based on a mixture of 'style'-structure and 'content' norms, thus the literary forms are numerated as: a. Oaths and related forms; b. Sign-passages; c. Say-passages; d. Narratives; e. Regulations; f. Liturgical forms and Others.[15]

15 See article 'Qur'ân', EI, vol. v, pp 400ff, section 7.

Muhammad Arkoun, though emphasizing the structure of the Qur'ân as a discourse, following Paul Ricoeur's typology of the Bible, which is based on the oriented definition of a text, distinguishes five types of discourse utilized in the Qur'ân, 'prophetic, legislative, narrative, sapiential and hymnal (poetic)'.[16] However, he maintains a notion of one structure of 'grammatical relations' and one 'realm of grammatical communication' defined in all Qur'ânic discourse.[17] Here the diversity and the multiplicity of the grammatical relations and the grammatical communications are reduced to one singular dominating structure.

The Qur'ân is the 'speech of God'; there is no dispute about this doctrine, but the discourse structure of the Qurân reveals multiplicity of voices not only one. As a discourse the Qur'ân is polyphonic not monophonic; there are so many voices in which the 'I' and/or 'We' speaker is not always the Divine voice. Sometimes the Divine voice is presented in the form of the third person 'He' or sometimes in the second person 'You'. The 'He' manifestation of the Divine preceded by the imperative "say" enunciated by another, probably unknown for certain, voice addressing Muhammad is to be found, for example, in chapter 112, one of the early chapters revealed in Mecca:

> *Say: He is Allah the One;*
> *Allah the Eternal Absolute;*
> *He begets not nor is He begotten;*
> *And there is none like Him*

According to the Islamic believe this unidentified voice should be the voice of Gabriel, the mediator and messenger of the Divine to reveal His message to Muhammad. As messenger he is explicating God's speech through his own voice acting on behalf of the Divine. Afterwards the implicit Divine voice, which became explicit to Muhammad via the angel's voice, has to be announced to the people, the target group of the message, via Muhammad's human voice. With all the involved three voices the mode of discourse in the chapter is the 'informative'.

16 Rethinking Islam, op cited, p.38.
17 ibid., pp. 38-39.

In the chronologically first revealed verses of the Qur'ân (1-5, chapter 96) where the addressee is obviously Muhammad, the voice of the speaker is the voice of the Angel who appeared to him at the cave of Hirâ'[18], for first time, or may be for the second time, introducing Muhammad to the Lord. The Lord is introduced in the third person. In this first enunciated discourse the angel voice does not seem explicating the Divine Voice; it is rather providing information about Him to Muhammad; the mode of discourse is 'informative'.

> *Recite, in the name of your Lord who creates*
> *Creates man from a clot.*
> *Recite; your Lord is the Most Bounteous,*
> *Who teaches by the pen,*
> *Teaches man that which he knew not.*

The report in the 'biography of the Prophet' through which we learn that Muhammad was hesitant to comply with the angel strong and repeated demand to 'recite' suggests that Muhammad might had been already involved in a certain 'recitation' in the name of certain divinity; the angel's voice demanding Muhammad to 'recite' seems to be aiming at convincing Muhammad to redress his recitation to the Lord presented. The structure of the discourse where the imperative 'recite' repeated twice supports this suggestion.

Moreover, in the hymn or/and the liturgical passages the voice of the speaker is the human voice and the addressee is the Divine being. The best example is the opening chapter of the Qur'ân to be recited in the five daily prayers which are obligatory for every Muslim.

> *Praise be to Allah the Lord of the Worlds.*
> *The Compassionate, the Merciful.*
> *Master of the Day of Judgment.*
> *It is You whom we worship and it is You from Whom we seek help*

---

18 According to the report narrated and related to the prophet on the account of his wife `Âisha, about the first encounter between Muhammad and the Holly Spirit, Gabriel, see, The Life of Muhammad (translation of Ibn Ishâq's Sîrat Rasûl Allâh) with introduction and notes by A. Guillaume, Pakistan Branch, Oxford University Press, Lahore, first published 1955, reprint 1967, p. 105

> *Guide us to the right course,*
> *The course of those whom You blessed,*
> *Not the course of whom provoked Your anger neither those who got astray.*

Interestingly, the recitation of this chapter is considered as invoking God's response, but while the recitation is explicit the Divine response is implicit. In other words, the recitor has to slowly recite the verses pausing to receive the answer. In other words, recitation of this chapter contains both vocalization and attentive hearing, *samâ`*. The following report is narrated as a (*qudsî*) hadith where God says:

> *salât is divided between Me and My servant into equal shares*
> *When he says, praise be to God, the Lord of the whole world,*
> *I say, My servant praised Me;*
> *When he says, The Compassionate The Merciful,*
> *I say, My servant exalted me;*
> *When he says, the Master of the Day of Judgment,*
> *I say, My servant glorified me;*
> *When he says, It is You whom we worship and it is You from Whom we seek help*
> *I say, this is between Me and My servant; all what My servant asked for is guaranteed;*
> *When he says, guide us to the right course, the course of those whom You blessed, not the course of whom provoked Your anger neither those who got astray,*
> *I say, these are for my servant and all are guaranteed for him.*[19]

This type of implicit dialogue between man and God, where man, although reciting God's speech, becomes the speaker, and God, the default Speaker of the 'recited' Qur'ân, becomes recipient, is very explicit in the structure of the Qur'ân. Within the polyphonic structure of the Qur'ânic discourse 'dialogue' is another characteristic to be presented.

---

19 See Al-Muwatta' by Mâlik b. Anas, kitâb al-nidâ' li-'salât, no. 174; Sahîh Muslim, kitâb al-salât, no. 598. Sakhr CD program Mawsû`at al-Hadîth al-Sharîf, Copyright Sakhr Software Co. 1995.

5- Dialogue

To mention frequented examples of 'dialoging' it is sufficient to refer to what is categorized as the 'say passages' where the structure 'they say … you say' exists. A 'dialogue' could be polemic, apologetic but it could be also inclusive or exclusive; it could be as well productive or destructive. We confine our self here to present three types of dialogue classified in terms of the addressee, the dialogue with unbelievers, that with the Jews and the Christians of Arabia and the dialogue with the believers.

The dialogue with the unbelievers, the polytheists of Mecca, started calm and soft, but gradually was hardened. When the pagan of Mecca started to negotiate with Muhammad, suggesting a way for Muhammad to show respect for their deities in exchange of recognizing his Lord, it seems in the context of the soft calm dialogue that Muhammad accepted. This brings the curious story mentioned in ancient historical sources which relates that Muhammad was reciting chapter 53 in the presence of a number of Meccan Polytheists and when he came to the names of three of their favorite deities mentioned in verses 19 and 20 two short verses were pronounced by Muhammad, 'they are the high-flying cranes (*gharânîq*) / whose intercession (with God) to be hoped for.' When the prophet reached in his recitation the last verse of the chapter, 'so prostrate yourselves before God and serve Him' the polytheists prostrated with Muslims in a signal of reconciliation between Muhammad and the Meccans.

Muslim scholars reject the story as a later invention while most European biographers of Muhammad accept it as historical. It is not our concern here to get involved in this debate, because the Qur'ân itself alludes to the story in chapter 22, verse 52, devaluating the validity of those two verses by attributing them to a satanic intrusion on Muhammad tongue, an intrusion to be deleted.

> *Never did We send an apostle or a prophet before thee, but, when he framed a desire, Satan threw some (vanity) into his desire: but God will cancel anything (vain) that Satan throws in, and God will confirm (and establish) His Signs: for God is full of Knowledge and Wisdom* (verse 52).

Whether this devaluation reflects a process of negotiation or not the fact remains that there is Qur'ânic evidence of the historical existence of the event, and this devaluation might be considered the first step of absolute demarcation between 'monotheism' and 'polytheism'. But this demarcation has to be set gradually.

First step was expressed in one of the early chapters, chapter 109, where Muhammad is advised, by the unknown voice - the angel's voice - not to negotiate with the unbelievers, the polytheists any more, but in the meantime to distance his conviction from theirs.

Say: O you who reject to believe!
I worship not that which you worship
Nor will you worship that which I worship.
And I will not worship that which ye have been worshipping
Nor will you worship that which I worship.
To you be your Way and to me mine.

Repetition of the phrase 'I worship not that which you worship' twice signifies the existence of strong opposition on the side of the unbelievers, accompanied with a strong repeated counter invitation to Muhammad for an exchange of worshipping. In other words, the style structure of that short chapter reveals the existence of dialogue in which the chapter is engaged.

But when an attack is launched against Muhammad and his prophetship is questioned the Qur'ân defends Muhammad. The people of Mecca contest the issue of the authenticity of the divine source of the Qur'ân, and therefore the issue of Muhammad's sincerity, honesty, trustworthy - his credibility - is challenged. The allegation that Muhammad forged and fabricated the Qur'ân is disputed and responded to not in the style form of 'they say', but it is understood from the refutation that it is a response. This is very characteristic of the 'discourse' structure, i.e., its involvement and engagement with another implicit, or explicit, discourse.

The Arabs tried every mean to explain the Qur'ânic unusual effect on them by explaining it in terms of all types of discourse known to them, discourses like 'soothsaying', poetry and even performing witchcraft. All their explanations were mentioned and refuted. When the

23

Arabs explain the nature of the Qur'ân as 'poetry' and accuse the prophet of composing it, the answer given to such an explanation and accusation is: "We have not taught him poetry; it is not seemly for him" (chapter 36:69). When they say that Muhammad is nothing but a soothsayer the Qur'ân replies: "By your Lord's blessing you are not a soothsayer neither possessed" (chapter 52:29). In the context of that debate the nonbelievers claimed that the Qur'ân was nothing but stories forged by Muhammad who claimed that they were revealed to him by God. They claimed that they were able to produce similar discourse. Facing such a challenge, the Qur'ân made its own counter challenge asking them to bring forth 'ten forged chapters like it' (chapter: 11:13).

When the nonbelievers failed to respond to this strong challenge, the Qur'ân, pretending to make it easier for them, decreased the challenge from 'ten' chapters to only 'one' (chapter 10:38). The last step was to indicate the absolute failure of the Arabs in challenging the authenticity of the Qur'ân:

> *"And if you are in doubt concerning that We have sent down on Our servant (Muhammad), then bring a chapter like it, and call your witnesses, apart from God, if you are truthful. And if you do not-and you will not- then fear the Fire, whose fuel is men and idols, prepared to unbelievers"* (chapter 2: 23-24).

This dispute and debate with the polytheist Arab grounded the development of the doctrine of *i`jâz*, the stylistic and literary incompatibility, or supremacy of the Qur'ân.

Another common form of the dialogue is the dialogue with the believers in the form "They will ask you [Muhammad] … you say" which is attested 15 times in the Qur'ân. These questions to which the Qur'ân responds cover different areas of interest. Questions were raised about wine and gambling (chapter 2:219), about the orphans (chapter 2:220), menstruation (chapter 2:222), dietary law (Chapter 5:4) charity (chapter 2:215,219), prohibition of fighting during the sacred month (chapter 2:217), and spoils of ware (chapter 8:1) Providing answers to such questions, much of the legal aspect of the Qur'ân was gradually articulated, thus reflecting the dialogical nature of the Qur'ân with the human interest.

Would the answers provided in the dialogical context be considered final legislation? What about different answers given to questions related to one issue? Lets take the example of intermarriage, which is one always provoked in any discussion about Human Rights in Islam. While in chapter 5:5 Muslims are allowed to marry non-Muslim females, such permission seems to be revoked in chapter 2:221. The question is which rule will prevail? The second question, which is only provoked in the modern age, is whether this permission is guaranteed only to male Muslim or should it be extended to the female as well?

Ibn Rushd tells us about two positions held by the jurists; the position of those who hold the permissibility considers 2:221 as presenting the general, the preference to marry a Muslim female, while 5:5 particularizes the general. The position of those who prohibit intermarriage is grounded on 'abrogation', i.e., that 2:221 abrogated 5:5.[20]

If we deal with the Qur'ân as discourse we can go far beyond the jurists' outlook that is motivated by law formulation that needs a certain mode of fixation. Each of the two verses is an independent discourse; while 2:221 reflects the non-negotiable stand with the polytheists, a position we earlier referred to, the verse of 5:5 is about 'togetherness' in social life. It is about 'making good things lawful'; it starts with 'food' indicating not only that the 'the food of the people of the book' is lawful to Muslims but that 'the food of Muslims' is lawful to the people of the book as well.

> *This day are (all) things good and pure made lawful unto you. The food of the People of the Book is lawful unto you and yours is lawful unto them.*

20 "The majority (of the jurists) upheld the permissibility of marriage with the kitâbiyyat (women of the people of the book) who are free (not slaves) through a contract, as the principle is to construe (by exemption) the particular from the general (=one of the principles of textual deduction). The words of the Exalted ... -(giving permission to marry women of the people of the book in 5:5)- is particular, while His words -(in 2:221 not to wed idolatress till they believe)- is general. Those (jurists) who inclined toward its prohibition, which is the opinion of some of the fuqahâ', jurists, considered the general meaning (in 5:5) to have abrogated the particular (in 2:221)" Ibn Rushd, Bidâyat al-Mujtahid wa Nihayat al-Muqtasid (A beginning for who is to be an independent jurist and a sufficient (source) for who is just seeking to learn not to be an expert), Vol. 11, p. 51.

This is a discourse about, first of 'good' things being lawful'; the first example of these 'good things' is sharing food. Intermarriage is introduced here as part of parcel of 'good things' which emphasizes the implicit call for social 'togetherness'.

> *Lawful unto you in marriage are chaste women who are believers as well as chaste women among the People of the Book revealed before your time when you give them their due dowers and desire chastity not lewdness nor secret intrigues. If anyone rejects faith fruitless is his work and in the Hereafter he will be in the ranks of those who have lost.*[21]

Addressing the modern question about equality in intermarriage, it suffices here to emphasize that the addressees of the Qur'ânic discourse in matters of marriage and divorce are males; it is after all a discourse which emerged in a patriarchal environment. Since the addressees are males, it is understandable that permission is voiced to men to marry, divorce, and marry off their relative females. If we recognize that, we are in a better position to enunciate that, according to paradigm-shift of meaning where equality is essential component, equality in intermarriage is possible.[22]

The justification provided by modern `ulamâ' to sustain the classical position could be easily negotiated. Addressing the modern question about equality in intermarriage, it suffices here to say that they still belief in the superiority of the male in the family affair, and accordingly they argue that the faith of non-Muslim women married to Muslim men will be respected. If a Muslim woman is married to

21 Chapter 5:5, and compare with 2:221 where another mode of discourse of no-negotiation with the polytheists is obvious "Do not marry unbelieving women (idolaters) until they believe; a slave woman who believes is better than an unbelieving woman even though she allure you. Nor marry (your girls) to unbelievers until they believe: a man slave who believes is better than unbeliever even though he allure you. Unbelievers do (but) beckon you to the fire. But Allah beckons by His grace to the Garden (of Bliss) and forgiveness and makes His Signs clear to mankind: that they may celebrate His praise.

22 The legal opinion provided by the European Council of Fatwâ to allow the continuation of the marriage for a newly converted Muslim female to her non-Muslim husband, which created a furious reaction in the Muslim World, was based on traditional early cases and justified on the wishful expectation that the guided wife will inspire the husband to convert.

non-Muslim, they fear that the non-Muslim husband will not respect the faith of his Muslim wife. They also invoked that Islam, being the last of God's revelations pays respect to both Judaism and Christianity, therefore, the faith of a non-Muslim woman married to a Muslim man is protected by the husband's faith. The reverse position is not possible, because Christianity does only recognize Judaism while Judaism recognizes neither Christianity nor Islam.

It is obvious that the `ulamâ' are still imprisoned in the patriarchal 'world vision' in one hand, and in the religious vision of the world on the other hand. Marriage decision is, or should be, the decision of the individual; it is her or his decision to set the condition she or he wants for the future life with spouse. The issue at stake is not so much intermarriage; it is rather the individual freedom that entails freedom of religion and belief. There is no time or space to address this issue here. It suffices to mention that there is no one single verse in the Qur'ân stipulating world punishment, or legal penalty, for apostasy; freedom of religion in the form of 'no coercion' is widely quoted even by the traditional `ulamâ', but in an apologetic manner.

6- Negotiation

As we have already shown the non-negotiation position with the polytheists brings about an exclusive mode of discourse; the only possible way of communication is dispute, debate and rejection. The discourse with the believers varies according to the way they handle their problem, according to their success they are praised; when they fail they are blamed and even condemned. This is also true for the Prophet himself. When he was busy preaching the rich people of Quraysh hoping that they would strengthen the newly formed community of believers, he did not pay attention to a poor blind fellow, identified as Ibn Umm Maktûm by the early exegete, who came asking for advice. The Qur'ân strongly blames Muhammad's attitude addressing him at the beginning by the third person, a sign of negligence.

He frowned and turned away
When the blind man came to him
What would make you know that he might elevate himself (if you
kindly responded to him)
Or be aware and such awareness brings him benefit
But as for whom who considers himself free from any need
To him you pay much attention
No blame on you if he would not elevate himself
As for who came to you striving (for knowledge)
While in fear (from God)
You did not pay attention to him! (Chapter 80:1-10)

The Qur'ânic discourse with the people of the book, the Jews and the Christians, or the *Nasârâ*, is the negotiate discourse par excellence. It is well known that the prophet Muhammad and his wife Khadîjah sought advice from a Christian Arab priest Waraqa b. Nawfal, who happened to be a cousin of Khadîjah. The matter of consultation was the first encounter with the Holy Spirit during the vision Muhammad had when he was meditating on mountain *Hirâ'*.[23]

It is also important to mention that the first Muslim migration *hijra* was to Abyssinia. In order to escape being persecuted by the people of Mecca, the Prophet ordered the Muslims to go there where, according to a statement related to the Prophet himself, "there is a Christian king who never does injustice to anyone." Muslims enjoyed his protection and hospitality till they returned back after the migration to Medina. During the period of their stay in Abyssinia, a delegation from Mecca visited the Emperor persuading him to send Muslims back to Mecca. The envoys of Mecca told the Negus that those who were enjoying his protection and generosity were only some rebels who protested against the religion of their own people's and converted to an unknown religion rather than to Christianity. In order to turn the Negus against Muslims he was told that they (the Muslims) blasphemed against Jesus Christ. When the Emperor asked the Muslim refugees about their belief concerning Jesus they read to him this passage of the Qur'ân from the chapter called 'Mary' or Maryam in Arabic (19).[24]

23 See the detailed account in The Life of Muhammad, op cited, pp. 106-7.
24 Ibid., pp. 146-152.

'Son of Mary' is one of the commonest titles given to Jesus in the Qur'ân in order to emphasize his human nature. Nevertheless, the Qur'ân also speaks of Jesus as 'a spirit from God' and 'His word caste into Mary' by the Holy Spirit. More than that: It was Jesus, according to the Qur'ân, who prophesied 'Ahmad' - Muhammad - to be the coming prophet.

> *And remember Jesus the son of Mary said: "O Children of Israel! I am the apostle of Allah (sent) to you confirming the Law (which came) before me and giving glad Tidings of an Apostle to come after me whose name shall be Ahmad." But when he came to them with Clear Signs they said "This is evident sorcery!"* (61.6)

It was only after migration to Medina that Muslims started actual contact with the Arab Jewish tribes who had long before come from Yemen and settled in Medina. The well known 'Medina Covenant' between the Prophet and both Jewish and pagan tribes clearly indicates an essential equality between all the peoples who lived in Medina. Liberty of religious practice was guaranteed on an equal footing as long as all the parties defended the security of the city against any outside attack or intrusion. Concerning different types of religious faith, equality was essentially guaranteed unless a war is initiated against Muslim, then the war conditions as historically practiced come into force.[25]

In this context the Qur'ân prescribed *siyâm*, fasting, for Muslims and in this also Muslims directed their prayers in the same direction as Jewish prayers, Jerusalem. But the relationship between the Muslim community and the Jewish community didn't continue as smoothly as it had started. Polemic dispute flared, engaging the Qur'ân which started to substitute the previous 'one religion' called 'Islam', that of all the prophets since Adam till Jesus:

> *1- Those who believed (in Muhammad), and those who became Jewish, and the Christians and the Sabian, any who believe in God and the last day, and do righteousness, shall have their reward from their Lord* (11:62, also 5:69.)

25 Ibid., the full text of the document pp. 231-233.

2- Those who believed (in Muhammad), and those who became Jewish, and the Sabians, Christians, Magians, and polytheists, God will judge between them on the Day of Judgment (22:17.)

3- Say (Mohammed), the truth comes down from God: Let him who will, believe, and let him who will, reject: for the wrong doers We have prepared a fire (18:29.)

4- He who will turn back from his faith, soon will God bring about (other) people whom He will love and they will love him (5:4.)

5- Those who reject faith after they accepted it, and then go in adding to their defiance of faith, never will their repentance be accepted; for they are those who have gone astray (3:90, also 4:137.)

The change of the praying direction for Muslims from Jerusalem to Mecca may indicate the first sign of demarcation between the two communities. The polemic dispute sometimes reaches the level of harsh condemnation. However, occasionally it is a type of quiet reminder of God's grace on the sons of Israel. This polemic dispute with its quiet as well its harsh manifestation can be followed in chapter 2, called 'the Cow', because it contains certain narrative reflecting the arrogance of the sons of Israel in complying with the simple demands of their prophets. There is a remarkable frequency in the use of the imperative 'remember' (some 19 times in chapter 2 alone), addressed directly to the sons of Israel preceding different narrative units of their history of reluctance and rejection to follow the right path.

Not being able to appreciate the 'discourse' structure it is likely to extend the discourse to be addressing all the Jews until the present. It is not only a question of contextualization, which is pivotal in discourse analysis, but more than that it is what the discourse tells about the context and how. Now, the question is which is historical and which is universal, a question that keeps all the modern liberal Muslim scholars of the Qur'ân busy. Being confined to the Qur'an as 'text' alone, the conservatives win at the end of the day. When the liberals, for example, emphasize 'togetherness' as the universal eliminating the 'hostility' limiting its meaning to the negative past the conservatives will apply the principal of 'abrogation' to historize 'togetherness' as abrogated and will universalize 'hostility', as the abrogat. In the present context of unsolved Palestinian-Israeli trauma, whose hermeneutics or meaning is valid? The winner is sure to be the meaning of ghetto, separation and isolation, the meaning of Mr. Sharon's wall.

The same is true about the polemic dispute with the Christians, the Nasârâ, about the nature of Jesus. We have shown already that the Qur'ân rendered Jesus prophesizing the coming of a prophet named Ahmad. And we have also seen how the chapter named Mary (19) was recited in the court of the Negus and in the presence of the bishops. A quick reading of this chapter and comparison with Matthew's Gospel will easily reveal common ground. Nevertheless, there is non-negotiable issue that maintains the boundaries between Muslims and Christians to the extent that the concept of 'togetherness' is almost forgotten.

The first issue is that of the human nature of Jesus according to the Qur'ân and the divine nature according to the shared dogma of the Churches. As we confine ourselves to the second chapter projecting the Qur'ânic discourse, or the Qur'ânic disputation with the Jews, we would also be better to confine our presentation to the Qur'ânic disputation with the *Nasârâ* to chapter three, which in its very opening, verse 3, advocates the credibility of all the revealed scriptures.

> *It is He Who sent down to thee (step by step) in truth the Book confirming what went before it; and He sent down Law (of Moses) and the Gospel (of Jesus) before this as a guide to mankind and He sent down the Criterion (of judgment between right and wrong).*

In verse four, however, it presents the possibility of misunderstanding as to keeping the shared ground as solid as possible. But we have to see the disputation context. While the Qur'ân recognizes Jesus as a 'word' from God (verse 45) and presents the Apostles as Muslims (52), it was clearly indicated in the earlier chapter of Mary, by way of relating to the child Jesus the statement 'I am the servant of God' (19:30). This seems to have caused certain confusion for the Christians of *Najrân* who came to Medina to debate with Muhammad.[26] The discussion

26 Ibid., pp. 270ff.

became heated, probably after it was explained that the miraculous birth of Jesus, from a mother who had not had intercourse with a male, makes him no different than Adam; the two cases are alike.

> *This similitude of Jesus before Allah is as that of Adam: He created him from dust then said to him: "Be" and he was* (3:59)

Then the Qur'ân made serious religious challenge that seems to cause fear among the delegation. Here we can realize the 'power' of discourse, or the discourse as 'authoritarian'; such a powerful discourse could not emerge in Mecca simply because Muslims were a small persecuted community. As the sources tells us the members of the Christian delegation withdrew preferring to pay annual collective amount of money *jizya* than face a possible curse as provoked by the Qur'ân.

> *If anyone disputes in this matter with you now after (full) knowledge has come to you say: "Come! let us gather together our sons and your sons our women and your women ourselves and yourselves: then let us earnestly pray and invoke the curse of Allah on those who lie!"* (3:61)

The non-negotiable issue for the Qur'ân was the divinity of Jesus, whether God or the Son; it is absolutely unacceptable just as there was no possible negotiation with the polytheist, hence the Qur'ân sometimes calls those who believe in Jesus' divinity either polytheist or unbelievers. So the only possibility of coming to terms with Christians is for them to relinquish their claim about Jesus, this being an impossible demand. The Qur'ân further cites the Christians' false arguments about things they do not know; the final truth is revealed to Muhammad. The claim of both the Jews and the Christians of being the only heirs of Abraham is shown to be false. The evidence shows this to be false: he was neither a Jew nor a Christian because both the Torah and the Gospel were revealed after his death (see 3: 64-67).

Now, the point I would like to indicate is that the Qur'ân never repudiated the Jewish and the Christian Scriptures; they are both revealed through the same channel as the Qur'ân: *wahy*. What is always disputed is the way the people of the book understood and explained these scriptures; the issue at stake is the wrong hermeneutics, and here comes the significance of the verse 7 in the same chapter 3, which was taken by Muslim theologians as setting hermeneutical principal. It reads

> *He it is Who has sent down to you the Book: in it are verses that are clearly expressed; they are the foundation of the Book: others are ambiguous. For those in whose hearts is perversity they follow (literally) the ambiguous seeking discord and searching for its hidden meanings but no one knows its hidden meanings except Allah and those who are firmly grounded in knowledge say: "We believe in the Book; the whole of it is from our Lord"; and none will grasp the Message except men of understanding.*[27]

My assessment here is that in the context of repudiating the Christian misunderstanding the verses in which the Qur'ân describes Jesus as the 'word' and the 'spirit' from God were declared 'ambiguous' whereas the verses emphasizing his humanity as only a prophet and messenger were declared the 'clear', the backbone of the book.

Another disputed issue between Muslims and Christians is the doctrine of crucifixion, which Muslims believe that the Qur'ân denies. Muslims see no conflict between normal death and ascension, both are asserted in the Qur'ân. Muslims see no conflict between the normal death of Jesus and his ascension; both are asserted in the Qur'ân. The context in which the issue of crucifixion is mentioned is not the context of a dispute with the Christians; it is the context of argumentation and disputation against the Jews in defense of Mary and Christ (4:153-158). In this context the Jewish blasphemous allegation of adultery against Mary is strongly repudiated and condemned by the Qur'ân. In

---

27 For a detailed discussion about the way this specific verse was isolated and, therefore, manipulated whether in terms of its grammatical articulation or in the meaning of its vocabularies and further more for the theological dispute, see Leah Kinberg art. 'ambiguous' EQ, vol. 1, pp. 70-76. Also my Al-ittijâh al-'Aqlî fî `Tafsîr: dirâsa fî mafhûm almajâz fî al-Qur'ân ind `l-Mu`tazila (the Rational Trend in Exegesis: study of the Mu`tazilites' concept of metaphor), op cited, pp. 180-9; Mafhûm al-Nass, op cited, pp. 179ff.

the same context the claim of the Jews that they slew Jesus, a claim implies a threat that they can also slay Muhammad, was also to be repudiated.

> *The people of the Book ask you to cause a book to descend to them from heaven: indeed they asked Moses for an even greater (miracle) for they said: "Show us Allah in public" but they were dazed for their presumption with thunder and lightning. Yet they worshipped the calf even after clear signs had come to them; even so We forgave them; and gave Moses manifest proofs of authority.*
>
> *And for their Covenant We raised over them (the towering height) of Mount (Sinai); and (on another occasion) We said: "Enter the gate with humility"; and (once again) We commanded them: "Transgress not in the matter of the Sabbath." And We took from them a solemn Covenant.*
>
> *(They have incurred divine displeasure): in that they broke their Covenant: that they rejected the Signs of Allah; that they slew the Messengers in defiance of right; that they said "Our hearts are the wrappings (which preserve Allah's Word; we need no more)"; nay Allah has set the seal on their hearts for their blasphemy and little is it they believe.*
>
> *That they rejected faith: that they uttered against Mary a grave false charge.*
>
> *That they said "We killed Christ Jesus the son of Mary the Apostle of Allah"; but they killed him not nor crucified him but so it was made to appear to them and those who differ therein are full of doubts with no (certain) knowledge but only conjecture to follow for of a surety they killed him not.*
>
> *Nay Allah raised him up unto Himself; and Allah is Exalted in Power Wise* (4:153-158).

If the issue of crucifixion was as important to the Qur'ân as the issue of the nature of Jesus, it would have been brought again and again in different contexts. Since it exists only in the context of responding to the Jewish claim, the discourse structure suggests it was denying the capability of the Jews to have done this depending on their own power, and by implication telling Muhammad that their implicit threat to slay him, as they slew Jesus, is not feasible, as God will not permit it. Now, once again the question is which meaning will prevail, togetherness or isolation? This duly brings the relationship of the West and the Muslim World into our discussion. How does relationship affect the way Muslims 'rethink' their own tradition so as to modernize their lives without relinquishing their spiritual power, particularly in view of America's colonizing project?

Now, let me present the possibility of real reformation in the domain of *sharî`a* if the concept of the Qur'ân is accepted.

7- Deconstructing Sharî`a

Would dealing with the Qur'ân as discourse, deeply involved in dialogue with the believers as well as with the non-believers, help us tackle the burning unsolved legal issues considered divine revelation by the majority of Muslims? Some radical groups may still be crying and fighting for the restoration of Caliphate, but the well-established national-state in every Muslim country in the post-colonial era has made a shift towards the question of law. The obligation to establish an Islamic state ruled entirely by *shari`a* is now the disputable issue between the two basic trends of modern Islamic discourse. That 'Islam is the official religion of the State and the principles of *sharî`a* are the source of legislation' is an article in the Constitution of all Muslim states.

The conflict sometimes taking the form of a severe and violent struggle between state and radical groups is not so much about whether or not *sharî`a* is to be implemented in both social and in individualistic life. It is much more about the degree of implementation and, so, if the political system is westernized or not and hence anti-Islamic.

If it is enough for the individual to confess Islam and to perform the other four pillars, praying five times a day, fasting the month of *Ramadân*, paying the annual prescribed alms, and performing *hajj* if it can possibly be financially afforded, for the community it is not enough. If an Islamic state is not established, every individual Muslim is responsible before God for such a religious failure; so preach the representatives of the radical Islamic groups and the representatives of the so-called 'moderate' Islamic discourse.

Muslim intellectuals, who hold different view about the relationship between Islam and politics, are condemned as 'westernized'; not real Muslim thinkers. The views of the non-traditional, nor radical, Muslim thinkers are not well known beyond the boundaries of the Muslim World, especially of those who prefer to address their readers in their own regional language. As for the highly radical, provocative preachers, the Western media is very keen to present their ideas, so creating the impression in the Western mind that Islam has but one face: the face of Ben Laden.

Let me present now briefly my scholarly view concerning the concept of *shari`a*. The Qur'ânic verses which seem to contain legal connotation and which are considered the basis of *shari`a* are about 500 verses according to the traditional sources. On these verses, which amount to one out of six, or 16% of the whole Qur'ân, the jurists built a system of induction and deduction called 'the principles of legislation', *`ilm usûl al-fiqh*. According to these principles, they added a second source to the Qur'ân, i.e., the Prophetic tradition, *al-sunna al-nabawiyya.* They categorized the *sunna* the second source of legislation and considered it as divine as the Qur'ân. As two divine sources were not enough to regulate the increasing political, social, economic as well as criminal problems, the jurists had to adopt a third principle based on the already agreed upon practiced legal rules called 'consensus', *ijmâ',* of the earliest Muslim generation, the companions of the Prophet (*al-sahâbah*). A fourth principal of 'rational inquiry', *ijtihâd*, was urgently needed in order to be able to solve the problems that were not solved in the other three sources. But this principle of *ijtihâd* was practically restricted to apply the technique of 'analogy', *qiyâs*, which is to reach a solution to a certain problem by only comparing its position to a similar problem previously solved by any of the three sources.

The whole body of *shari`a* literature, as expressed in the major four sunni schools, *madhhabs*, at least, is built on the aforementioned principles, which means that *shari`a* is a man-made production; nothing is divine about it. It is neither possible to claim its validity regardless of time and space.

If we contextually examine some of the Qur'anic legal stipulations, such as the penalty of fornication, *zinâ*, robbery, *sariqah*, or causing social disorder, *hirâbah*, as well as slaying, *qatl*, which are called *hudûd*, pl. of *hadd*, the question is: are these penalties basically initiated by Islam, and, therefore, Islamic? The answer is definitely 'no'; all these penalties were generally pre-Islamic, some of them belong to the Roman law and adopted in the Jewish tradition, while others were even older tradition. It is not likely in our modern age of Human Rights and respect of the integrity of the human being to consider amputation of the members of the human body, or execution, as obligatory religious punishments binding by divinity.

Other aspects of *shari`a*, such as those dealing with the rights of religious minorities, women's rights, and Human Rights in general, have to be revised and reconsidered as well. Contextualization of the Qur'ânic stipulation, and examining its linguistic and stylistic structure -as discourse- would reveal that the jurists' work was basically to unfold the meaning of such stipulation and to re-encode such meaning in their different social contexts. The Qur'ân is not in itself a book of law; legal stipulations are expressed, as we have already proved, in discourse style, which reveal a context of engagement with human needs in specific time, which, in turns, opens up the appropriation of the 'meaning' intended into every paradigm of meaning.

As discourse it provides multi-options, various solutions, and open gate of understanding. The conclusion is that to claim that the body of *shari`a* literature is binding for all Muslim communities regardless of time and space is simply ascribing divinity to human historical production of thought. If this is the case, there is no obligation to establish a theocratic state claimed Islamic. Such a demand is nothing but ideological call to establish a theo-political unquestionable authority; it is the recreation of the most devilish dictatorship political regime on the expense of the spiritual and ethical dimension of Islam.

8-The Challenge of Modernity: confusing context

Muslims so far have been rethinking, redefining and modifying the sources of Islamic knowledge. Traditions such as Sunna, consensus and legal syllogisms have been under deep and controversial discussion and debate since the eighteenth century. The meaning of the

Qur'ân, and subsequently the meaning of Islam, has been the subject of investigation, research, appropriation, re-appropriation and negotiation since the late nineteenth century. This type of 'rethinking' was essentially and initially motivated by a strong commitment to develop Muslim societies in the direction of modernization on one hand, and to keep the spirit of Islam and its forces alive on the other hand; modernity was, after all, a foreign power imposed from above by the colonial European domination of the entire Muslim World after deconstructing the Ottoman Empire.

By the end of the nineteenth century, the British had successfully colonized much of India. The French, under Napoleon Bonaparte, occupied Egypt in 1798. France then went into Algeria in 1830; occupied Tunisia in 1881, and Britain marched into Egypt in 1882. The Dutch were already there long before that in Indonesia. There were many other excursions as the West's program of the colonization unfolded throughout the Muslim World.

Here one can mention at least three challenging powers that motivated and constructed the way Muslims rethought their traditions. First of all, it was the challenge of scientific discoveries and the advanced technology. The second challenging question was the question of rationality and rationalism whereas the third was the political challenge. Needless to say these three challenging questions, presented here independently, were always mixed in each one of the exegesis' trends we are going to present.

1- Modern science and technology were introduced to the Muslim world in the form of strange unknown military equipment that caused their defeat against the empirical Western powers and lead to the occupation of their land by non-Muslim invaders. When the French army reached Alexandria in 1798 the Mamlûk worriers were ready to fight in man-to-man combat. However, they were shocked to see the powerful artillery machines that killed dozens of soldiers with one shot, from a long distance. Napoleon Bonaparte brought with his army a number of natural and social scientists. Al-Jabartî in his history tells of the reaction of the Azharî `ulamâ' when they were invited to watch some chemical experiments performed for them in the laboratory established in Cairo. They were terrified, some of them ran away whispering the *isti`adha* formula (seeking God's protection from devil), because they perceived these experiments as witchcraft. That was the first encounter of Egyptian intellectuals with modern technology courtesy of modern scientific investigation and research. Their response was to learn in order to gain the power to be able to fight back. Learning modern sciences, by sending missions of students to acquire the sciences in Europe, and importing modern technology, especially military weapons - this was the basic response by both Turkey and Egypt.

2- Within the military power there was an intellectual weapon holding Islam responsible for the weakness of the Muslim world. In this context the Muslim World was perceived, approached and addressed by the colonizer's mentality as Muslim, with no other sub-identity attached, like Indian, Indonesian or Arab. The matter became more complicated when the colonized unquestionably accepted the identity imposed on them by the colonizer, and by way of internalization reduced their identity, thus, creating an identity crisis.

It was explicitly advocated that it was necessary to neglect and even abandon Islam, if this part of the world was to make any progress toward catching with modernity. It is enough to mention the French philosopher Ernest Renan (1832-1892) and the French politician and historian Gabriel Hanotaux (1853-1944)[28], who served as Minister of Foreign Affairs from 1894 to 1898. Renan posited the absolute incompatibility between Islam and both sciences and philosophy. Whatever is labeled Islamic science or Islamic philosophy is, according to Renan in his doctoral thesis, *Averroès et l'Averroïsme* (1852; "Averroës and Averroism"), mere translation from the Greek. Islam, like all religious dogmas built on revelation, is hostile to reason and freethinking. Hanotaux too held Islam responsible for the backwardness of the Muslim world. His allegation was based on the theological difference between Islam and Christianity.

---

28 A statesman, diplomat, and historian who directed a major French colonial expansion in Africa and who championed a Franco-Russian alliance that proved important in the events leading to World War I. As a French nationalist he was committed to policies of colonial expansion. During his ministry, French domination was established in French West Africa, Madagascar, and Tunisia; inroads were made in Algeria.

According to him the dogma of incarnation in Christianity has its consequence in building a bridge between man and God, thus freeing man from any dogma of determinism. Islamic pure monotheism, *tawhîd*, on the other hand, has created a non-bridged distance between man and God, leaving no space for human free will. By such theological reason Hanotoux explained the political despotism characterizing the Muslim World.[29]

Jamâl al-Dîn al-Afghânî (1838-1897)[30] and Muhammad Abdu (1848-1905) responded defensively, relating the backwardness of Muslims not to Islam per se, but to the contemporary Muslims' misunderstanding of Islam. They both argue, if Islam is understood properly and explained correctly, as was the case in the golden age of Islamic civilization, Muslims would not have been easily defeated, and dominated by European power.

The basic question that confronted the early modern Muslim reformers was whether Islam is compatible with modernity or not. How could a faithful Muslim live in a modern socio-political environment, without losing her/his identity as a Muslim? Does Islam accommodate science and philosophy? Second came the question of the compatibility or otherwise of the divine law (*shari'a*) that constitutes traditional society, and the positive law that constitutes the modern nation-state. Were modern political institutions such as democracy, elections, and parliament accepted by Islam, and could they replace the traditional institutions of *shûrâ*, consultation, and the authority of the elite 'ulama (*ahl al-hall wa al-'aqd*)?

3- The discussion of such questions are embedded in the question of religion and politics. The issue of political Islam emerged under the colonial occupation of most of the Muslim countries as early as 1798

29 See the translation of Hanotaux article into Arabic and Muhammad `Abdu's response in Al-A`mâl al-Kâmilah lil Imâm Muhammad `Abdu, (the Complete Works of Imâm Muhammad `Abdu) ed. Muhammad `Amârah, 5 vols, Beirut 1972 v. 5, p. 201f

30 Extensive information on al-Afghani can be found in N. Keddie, An Islamic Response to Imperialism: Political and Religious Writings of Sayyid Jamal ad-Din al-Afghani (Berkeley, 1983); R. Matthee, 'Jamal al-Din al-Afghani and the Egyptian National Debate', IJMES, Vol. 21 (1989), pp. 151-169; E. Kedourie, 'Afghani and Abduh. An Essay on Religious Unbelief and Political Activism', Modern Islam (London, 1966).

in Egypt for example, where Muslims became aware of different lifestyle brought about in their everyday life by their colonizers. They look and dress differently, behave and speak differently. They eat *harâm* food, drink wine, interact freely with women who are not their *mahram*, even their women are dressed improperly. In brief, Muslim social and religious identity was extremely violated by the very existence of those intruders in otherwise purely Muslim territory.

Ironically, or paradoxically may be, that Bonaparte presented himself to the Egyptian `ulamâ'as the protector of 'faith' against both the Catholic Pope and the corrupted Ottoman Sultan. Then he advanced his claim pretending that he converted to Islam. Nothing of this worked out. The issue of politics emerged after the collapse of the Ottoman Empire with the end of the First World War. The decision of the new national Turkish movement to abolish Caliphate raised the question whether Caliphate was an Islamic institution or was only a form of political system that could be replaced by another without losing the identity of Islam. Amidst such state of stress and uncertainty in such transitional period the Muslim world found itself suddenly stripped of its identity, namely the Caliphate. Political figures, such as King Fu'âd in Egypt and Sharief Husayn in Arabia, tried to restore Caliphate, with each seeking to be nominated as Caliph of all Muslims.

It was the Egyptian `Alî `Abd al-Râziq (1888-1966) who defended the abolishment of Caliphate proving that there is no such a specific political system labeled Islamic. The response of Muhammad Rashîd Rida (1865-1935) was different. He defended Caliphate as an authentic Islamic system that should be re-established, failing which Muslims would suffer the return to paganism, *jâhiliyya*.[31] As

---

31 Meaning paganism, in reference to the pre-Islamic tribal cultural code in Arabia translated sometimes as ignorance. Rida was very much in favor of the Wahhâbî ideology based on the writings of Muhammed b. `Abd al-Wahhâb (d. 1135/1792) who was himself a follower of the most Orthodox Muslim thinker, Ibn Taymiyya (d.685/1328). As Rida was a traditionalist thinker he inspired Hasan al-Bannâ that it is possible to establish the Caliphate state. The successful example set by both M. b. Abdul Wahhâb and Muhammâd b. Su`ûd in establishing a theocratic state to be the kingdom of God was alive. The dream of both the ideologist and the ambitious Prince became true by embodying the ideology in militant body of tribes called ikhwân. Muslim Brotherhood Society was formed in order to be the embryo of the future Islamic State of Egypt.

a political response the Muslim Brotherhood Society was established in Egypt in 1928. Its basic aim was to re-establish Islamic society in Egypt as an ideal example to be copied everywhere before the re-establishment of Caliphate. Hence re-islamization became thus the antonym of modernization, which was presented as westernization. The modern political islamist movements, labeled usually as fundamentalism in Western public discourse, are all off-shoots of the Muslim Brotherhood Society.

In such a historical and confusing context, the question of the 'nature' of the Qur'ân, its 'structure' as well as its historical background, was never closely dealt with. As the foundational text of Islam per excellence it was kept above any critical investigation; it was the only preserved cardinal and fundamental source of inspiration to hold on; it is, first and last of all, the verbatim speech of God. Muslims perceived the Orientalist's scholarship about the Qur'ân, its history and structure as part of the European conspiracy against Islam and Muslims.

9- Rethinking Tradition

To start with I would like to briefly present the other non-violent, more open and probably liberal face of modern Islam known only to the sincere and non-biased scholars, a face somewhat hidden and a voice quite mute in the mass Media of East and West alike. From this presentation, the question of 'rethinking the Qur'ân' will, I hope, emerge as vital if Muslims really wish to follow up the essential basic project of modernization, with more constructive participation.

In order to give a brief account of this process one has to outline the epistemological principles of Classical Islam as it reached the modern age and had to be rethought. Let me clarify that the four sources to be outlined here represent only one facet of the multi-faceted Islamic culture, i.e., the facet of jurisprudence, *sharî`a*. They present the epistemological principles called (*usûl al-fiqh*) from which the normative law, *fiqh*, is deduced. All the revivalist movements were to a great extent directed by the state of affairs in which Islam came to be fixed, that is Islam as law-oriented (*sharî`a*) faith. Scholars of Islam know *shari`a* is one of the multi-facets of the

Islamic traditions and cultures, one that can be distinguished from at least other several facets, such as philosophy, theology (`ilm al-kalâm`), Sufism, etc.

The reason behind reducing Islam to the paradigm of *shari`a* is the fact that since the fifth century of the Islamic era, i.e. the twelfth century, Islamic philosophy and Islamic theology as well as the creative philosophy of Sufism have been gradually marginalized. Philosophers and non-orthodox theologians, such as the well-known Ibn Rushd, suffered various degrees of persecution. Indeed, great sufîs, such as al-Hallâj (exc. 910) and Suhrawardî (Shihâb al-Dîn Yahya, exc. 1191) to mention only two names, were executed. In terms of their hierarchal order the sources of knowledge, according to major schools of law, are arranged as follow:

First and foremost, the Qur'ân and its exegesis present the foundational treasure of knowledge; it is the Speech of God revealed in Arabic to prophet Muhammad in the seventh century. Though basically addressing the Arabs, its message is meant for all humanity regardless of time and space. This is the guidance, the light, and the final divine plan for salvation in this world as well as in the life to come.

Second to the Qur'ân are the sayings and the actions of the prophet Muhammad, including his approval or disapproval of sayings or actions of his companions. This is the prophetic tradition known in Arabic as Sunna. It came to be considered equally divine with the Qur'ân because both are revelations from God. The difference between them was explained in terms of differentiating between the 'content' and the linguistic expression or the 'form' of both. The Qur'ân is God's verbatim speech, so its content and its linguistic expression (form) are both divine. The content of the Sunna, on the other hand, is revealed, meaning divine, but its form is human; Muhammad put it into words. Nevertheless, its position is not inferior to the Qur'ân; it is equal though secondary. Muslim jurists even emphasized that the Qur'ân is in need of the Sunna more than the Sunna is in need of the Qur'ân. The Sunna is not only to explain but more to explicate what is implicit, such as how to perform prayer and fasting, or to know the conditions of purification and the amount of alms to be paid etc. Without the Sunna the Qur'ân is less clear. Even to understand the context of the passages and chapters of the Qur'ân, the historical events that surrounded the revelation - a process lasting more than twenty years - only the Sunna can provide such (historical) information.

The third epistemological principle or source of knowledge is the 'consensus' of the community of scholars, `ulamâ'. As there was no *consensus* among the scholars on the epistemological validity of the doctrine of 'consensus', neither could there be an agreement on its definition and the final formulation limited its scope as well as its implication. Its scope was narrowed to refer only to what was unanimously agreed upon among the first Muslim generation, the Companions of the Prophet, *sahâba*, on the assumption that such consensus should had been grounded on certain prophetic tradition that was not transmitted to the next generation. Consequently, its implication was limited to issues not mentioned, either explicitly or implicitly, in the above two sources.[32]

The fourth and last source of acquiring knowledge is the application of rational syllogisms, inferring a rule for a certain non-mentioned case in the sources above by way of making analogy with a similar established rule. The analogy is to be based either on similarity, like the similarity between consuming alcohol and smoking hash, or on the rationale of the rule mentioned. The second type of analogy requires adherence to the theological doctrine of the existence of 'rational logic' behind God's divine rules, a doctrine that was not accepted by all schools of law. Unlike 'consensus' *qiyâs*, though was not applied by all the jurists, gained more support by the majority.[33]

10-Rethinking Consensus: the emergence of new `ulamâ'

It seems that the process of 'rethinking' tradition, which started as response to the degeneration position into which Muslim societies were falling, took its first step with the third principle, namely consensus; it was easy to break through by demanding a new type of consensus. Shâh Walî Allâh (1702-1762) is considered the godfather of the 'revivalist' Islam in India. Due to the specific orientation of the Indian Islam, his revivalist formula was a combination of 'sufism' and

32 See, Bernard, M., article 'Ijmâ'' in EI, vol. 111, pp. 1023f.'
33 See, Bernard, M, article 'qiyâs' in EI, vol. v, pp. 238.

*shari`a* oriented thought. In contrast to the Wahabî movement in Arabia, initiated by Muhammad b. `Abd al-Wahâb (1703-1792) which took the direction of a highly Orthodox reformation, it is possible to explain the differences in line with the different historical and cultural background of Islam, in both social environments. While Islam in India was reshaped by its interaction with pre-Islamic Indian tradition, such as Hinduism Buddhism, Islam in Arabia was to a great extent rooted in its Bedouin tradition and customs.

Shah Walî Allah, heavily influenced by the breakdown of the Mugal authority which led to the loss of Muslim power, sought to encourage the revival of a strong central authority by invoking a concept of two complementary authorities, two caliphates, one is political and the other is juridical, both are responsible for the preservation of Islam. For the political authority he uses the term *zâhir*, meaning external, and to this he assigns the responsibility for maintaining administrative and political order and for applying the *Shari`a*. For the juridical he employs the term *bâtin*, internal, and its responsibility is to give guidance to the religious leaders of the community, a role that Shah Walî Allah took upon himself.[34]

The similarity between this approach and that of Ibn `Abd al-Wahhâb is obvious, bringing together the political authority and the authority of the jurist, *faqîh*, to work toward the restoration of Islam from its state of decadence. The difference between the two approaches remains in this sufi tone that is characteristic of Indian Islam.

Within this sufi tone, and in order to establish the position of the jurist as partner in the state affair, Shah Walî Allah was able to be critical of the Classical structure of *shari`a*; he was able to reject *taqlîd*, the uncritical adherence to the opinions of the `*ulamâ*' of the Classical schools of law, and a revival of interest in the use of personal effort to decide a point of law, *ijtihâd* by employing *qiyâs*. By such a revival of the principle of personal understanding Shah Walî Allah was able to bypass the history of stagnation in the field of *shari`a* scholarship.

He emphasized the spirit of law, which is applicable in all times and places, rather than the form of law, which is shaped and formulated in accordance with conditions of time and place. Not only does

---

34 See Brown, Daniel, *Rethinking Tradition in Modern Islamic Thought*, Cambridge Middle East Studies, Cambridge University Press, UK 1996, pp. 22-3.

he revive the concept of *maslaha*,[35] the community interest, from the *Mâlikî*'s school of law, but he basically and initially depends on the well-established Sufi distinction between *shari`a* and *haqîqa*, where the first is considered historical and limited in time and space while the later is the Truth attained by spiritual exercise that leads to vision of Reality.

As a jurist sufi, he tried to cleanse Sunna from any theological influence, because theology presents an imposition of rational contemplation on matters that are either clearly indicated in the Scripture (the Qur'ân and the Tradition of the Prophet, Sunna) or matters that are not mentioned in any. Sunna, according to him, is, on the contrary, the agreed upon practice of the Muslim community. By such a distinction, he successfully dissociated Sunna from theology which, according to him, caused the People of the *Qibla* (Muslims) to become separate sects and destined factions beyond their following the essentials of religion.[36]

While, as we shall see, early Indian revivalist discourse presented by Shah Walî Allah encouraged later development, Wahhâbism has never developed away from the basic ideas first formulated by the founder. The absolute unity between dogma and political regime offered no scope for political opposition, but advocated more radical and fundamentalist ideologies. Now, in the context of the American pressure to reshape the whole Arab world politically and intellectually, there are a lot of gatherings, conferences, etc. basically aiming to represent Wahhâbism as a liberal, open and democratic system. It is an attempt to apply some makeup to the same old face.

In Egypt a similar revivalist, but probably more liberal approach, appeared after the first encounter with Europe. Shaykh, Refâ`a Râfi` al-Tahtâwî (1801-1873) was sent to act as an *imâm* for the first Egyptian military mission to France (to acquire modern military training). He was very much inspired by his teacher Hasan al-`Attâr, the rector of al-Azhar for five years (1830-1834) who tried to introduce secular sciences to the curriculum of the oldest Islamic educational institution in Egypt, al-Azhar. Paradoxically, the objection

---

35 Hujjat Allâh al-Bâligha (The Conclusive Argument from God), translated by H. Daiber and D, Pringree, EJ. Beill 1996, p.11.
36 ibid., p. 24.

came from the French director of the school of medicine in Cairo on the grounds that al-Azhar should continue as an exclusively religious institution. Shaykh Hasan al-`Attâr, being himself well versed in secular sciences including astronomy, medicine, chemistry, and engineering, as well as literature and music, found no contradiction between religious knowledge and secular disciplines.[37]

Inspired by such a master, Tahtâwî managed to learn French and to read some of the eighteenth century French thought and literature. Perhaps more importantly he had time to see and observe everyday life in Paris and to record his observations in a book that was published after his return to Egypt, entitled *Takhlîs al-Ibrîz fî Talkhîs Pariz* (Summary of Paris). On his return he was appointed director of the newly established School of Languages (*Madrasat al-Alsun*). A bureau of translation was attached to the school in 1841. Books were translated to and from various (European) languages, covering the fields of geography, history, geometry, mathematics, engineering, law, etc. In addition to all these duties, he was appointed the chief editor of the first official newspaper *al-Waqâi` al-Misriyyah*.[38]

Al-Tahtâwî's contribution to the study of Islam and 'rethinking tradition', besides being a pioneer in the intellectual awakening process, relies in the fact that he gives a new turn to the idea of the `ulama'. In his view, they are not simply guardians of a fixed and established tradition. Himself well versed in the religious law, as Shâfi`î by legal rite, he believed it was necessary to adapt *sharî`a* to new circumstances and that it was legitimate to do so. Very much like Shah Walî Allah, he provoked the reopening of the gate of *`ijtihâd*, which had been announced closed. He even went one step further to suggest that there was not much difference, he suggested, between the principles of *sharî`a* and the principles of 'natural law' on which the codes of modern Europe were based. This suggestion implied that Islamic law could be reinterpreted in the direction of conformity with modern needs, and he suggested a principle which could be used to justify this: that it is legitimate for a believer, in certain circumstances, to accept an

---

37 See "the Report on the Religious Condition in Egypt (Taqrîr al-Hallah al-DIniyyah fI Misr), al-Ahrâm Centre for Political and Strategic Studies, Cairo 1995.

38 Hourani, Albert, Arabic Thought in the liberal Age (1798-1939), Cambridge Universitry Press, London 1983, reprinted 1984, p. 71).

interpretation of the law drawn from a legal code other than his own. Taken up by later writers, this suggestion was used in the creation of a modern and uniform system of Islamic law in Egypt and elsewhere.[39]

It is worth noting that the Muslim reformists were able to break through the principle of consensus by re-invoking the principle of rational reasoning, *ijtihâd*, which was quite feasible and successful, by supporting the fourth principle, i.e. legal syllogisms, *qiyâs*. By undermining the principle of 'consensus', they were able to navigate through the volumes of law, *fiqh*, without limiting themselves to following a specific school, which gave them more freedom to choose opinions and to build legal syllogisms. This type of reformation became instrumental in the field of law formulation and sharî`a codification in so many Muslim countries.

The process of breaking 'consensus' continued to present the major development throughout the twentieth century. A new class of intellectuals started to be engaged, challenging the hegemonic authority of the traditional class of `ulamâ' across the Muslim World, thanks to the age of print and the press, and the introduction of modern educational systems. All these were essential elements in the process of building the post-independence nation states. Now, with the intensive use of Internet, the traditional authority of the `ulamâ' and even the authority of modern intellectuals has been fragmented. If the traditional `ulamâ' were the ones who challenged and rethought the principle of 'consensus', thus, opening new space of rational reflection on Tradition, it was for the new emerging class of intellectuals to go a step further in the process of 'rethinking'.[40]

11- Rethinking Sunna, hadith criticism: the emergence of new exegesis

As explained earlier Sunna encompasses the sayings and actions of the prophet Muhammad as well as his approval and/or disapproval of his companions' sayings and actions. Unlike the Qur'ân that was recorded down in written form early, Sunna was orally transmitted

39 Hourani, op. cited. p. 75.
40 See, Dale F. Eickelman and Jon W. Anderson (eds.) New Media in the Muslim World, Indiana University Press, 1999, especially their contributions and the introduction.

before the compellation of the collections of Tradition around the end of second/eighth century. The fact that all the reports containing tradition were orally transmitted with the possibility of fabrication for various reasons and motivations, made the early scholars of hadîth who were very aware of the possibility,– develop certain critical rules to evaluate authenticity, and hence what was to be accepted, and to avoid fabrications entering the collections.

This traditional hadîth criticism approach was re-invoked and even developed beyond its traditional critical paradigm in the modern context of 'rethinking'. Rethinking the Sunna was associated with the efforts to reopen the meaning of the Qur'ân to address modern issues by way of trying to establish a new Qur'ânic exegesis, void of the heavy classical reliance on Tradition in the classical commentaries of the Qur'ân. In other words, the criticism of Sunna was basically one of the results of the Muslim thinkers being involved in Qur'ânic exegesis in a rather different way than that of the classical exegetes. The strong demand for a new approach in dealing with the Qur'ân in order to open its meaning for the new challenging circumstances made it essential to distance modern Qur'ânic exegesis from the traditional type heavily loaded with hadith quotations.

Sir Sayyed Ahmad Khân of India (1817-1898) [41], not a traditional `âlim, was the first Indian modernist to introduce new themes, hitherto unknown in this interpretation. An apologist, he tried to justify the religious dogmas presented in the Qur'ân in the light of modern scientific discoveries. The perception that the Qur'ân should occupy the central place in guiding the behavior of the Muslims, as against the dominant role of the Prophetic traditions generally accepted by the `ulamâ', was apparently gaining popularity among a section of Muslim intelligentsia during late nineteenth and early twentieth centuries in India. This was intended primarily to create space for the interpretation of the Qur'ân in modern terms, and also to eradicate superstitions prevalent in Muslim societies. Sayyed Ahmad was the first to have raised this issue. He points to anomalies in the interpretation of the Qur'ân and suggests that these are void of

41 On Sir Sayyad Ahmad Khân, see Christian W. Troll, Sayyid Ahmad Khân: An Interpretation of Muslim Theory (Oxford University Press, New Delhi, 1978); Hafeez Malik, Sir sayyid Ahmad Khân and Muslim Modernization in India and Pakistan (Columbia University Press, New York, 1980).

even general principles on which to base an understanding of the Holy Scripture. Most of what the classical commentators have provided only concern derivations from the Qur'ân of canon law, scholastic theology, admonitions and similar other matters. Not a few parts of the classical commentaries are "worthless and full of weak and fabricated (Prophetic) traditions" or comprise baseless stories borrowed from Judaism.

It is imperative, therefore, for him to free the field of Qurânic exegesis from tradition, substituting instead the principles of 'reason' and 'nature'. He proposes that the Qur'ân stands on its own, requiring only application of a dedicated and enlightened mind for its understanding. The principles of interpretation, according to Ahmad Khân, should not depend on hadîth otherwise the eternal and universal quality of the Qur'ân will be put at risk. For him, the great miracle of the Qur'ân is its universality which makes it possible for every generation to find in it the meaning relevant to its situation, despite the constant increase in human knowledge. Hadîth-based interpretation tends to limit the meaning of the Qur'ân to a particular historical situation, thus obscuring its universality.[42]

This approach led Ahmad Khân to the critical approach to the second source of Islamic knowledge, the Sunna. Under the influence of Biblical criticism applied to the transmission of hadîth's reports by European scholars like Carl Pfander (1803-1865) and William Muir (1819-1905) on one hand, and in response to the close-minded, Wahhâbî oriented, attitude developed by Ahl-i-Hadîth, on the other hand, he "eventually came to reject almost all hadîth as unreliable".[43] But his refutation of hadîth does not mean that he rejects Sunna altogether, although hadîth is considered to be the major carrier of Sunna.

Like Ahmad Khân, the Egyptian Muhammad Abdu (1848-1905) seems to have a critical, though more cautious, attitude towards the material that had been handed down in the canonized collections of Sunna. He did not theoretically elaborate on redefining the authentic Tradition; but he occasionally refutes traditions that contradict either the explicit meaning of a certain Qur'ânic passages or both reason and commonsense. This is obviously shown in his rejection of the

42 Rethinking Tradition, cited, p. 44.
43 Ibid., p. 33.

traditions related to magic or the satanic touch, as well as those mentioning the angels descending to fight the enemy alongside the Muslim warriors. As we will see, his semi-rational interpretation of the Qur'an, necessitates a critical approach to tradition.[44]

The early twentieth century witnessed the emergence of Ahl-i-Qur'ân movement in India as a critical response to the emphasis laid on the authority of Sunna by Ahl-i-Hadîth group, an emphasis which resulted in leaning towards a ritualistic version of reformation. The basic challenge presented by Ahl-i-Qur'ân was not the authenticity of Sunna as transmitted through hadîth reports, but it was basically whether the Sunna stands in the same position of the Qur'ân as divine revelation. The Classical position holding Sunna as a form of revelation equal to the Qur'ân in authority, though different in its form, was challenged.

Similar controversy, though less violent in tone than in India, was also happening in Egypt. Just as the Indian Ahl-i-Qur'ân were influenced by Sayyid Ahmad Khân's emphasis on the Qur'ânic universalism versus the Sunna historicity, so the Egyptian critics of Sunna developed `Abdu's cautious attitude toward hadîth literature into a more radical attitude raising the slogan 'Islam is the Qur'ân alone' in a series of articles in al-Manâr in 1907.[45] There was strong reaction against this claim from several Muslim countries including one from India.[46] One of the more interesting outcomes of discussion around the authenticity of hadîth has been the emergence of attempts to separate the question of the authority of sunna from the problem of the historical authenticity of hadîth criticism - to accept the results of modern hadîth criticism, at least in part, while in principle preserving the authenticity of sunna.

This was the general approach to sunna promoted by the Lahore based Institute of Islamic Culture.[47] A similar but much more sophisticated attempt to separate the authority of sunna from the strict authenticity of hadîth is found in the work of the Pakistani modernist Fazlur Rahman (1919-1988), who served as director of Pakistan's Central Institute for Islamic Research in the 1960s.

44 Ibid., p.37.
45 These articles were written by Muhammad Tawfîq Sidqî, al-Manâr, v. 7, pp. 515-525; v. 10, pp 683-689; v.11, pp. 689-697 and 717-779.
46 Ibid., v. 11,141-145 and 521-527
47 Rethinking Tradition, op cited, pp. 100-1.

This institute was established by the regime of General Ayyûb Khân to help promotion of modernist interpretations of Islam compatible with the needs of the regime. Fazlur Rahman's works on sunna must be understood against the background of religious politics in Pakistan during the 1960s and, in particular, against the background of the controversy between Ghulâm Ahmad Parwēz (one of Ahli-i-Qur'ân group) and his opponents among the Pakistani `ulamâ'. Parwēz's radical rejection of sunna and his particular vision of Islamic state as true heir of Prophetic authority[48] was associated in the minds of his opponents with the efforts of the Ayyûb government to bypass the `ulamâ' in order to promote modernist Islam.

Opponents of the government suspected, quite correctly, that Ayyûb was intent on bypassing the traditional sources of religious authority in his formulation of policy. They concluded, probably incorrectly, that Parwēz's ideas were exercising an undue effect on government policy. Thus the debate over the relationship between religion and state and the relative rule of the `ulamâ' and the government in formulating policy on religious question became focused on Parwēz's ideas, and particularly on the issue of Sunna. Attention was also focused on the regime's major voice in religious matters, the Central Institute of Islamic Research and its director.[49]

The story of the institute and its rule in the state structure in Pakistân is worth mentioning; it shows how instrumental the criticism of Sunna was for the process of formulating modern law. It shows also the failure of the reformation movement when it is too connected to the pragmatic policy of the political regimes. The example of Pakistân could be found in different degree in other Muslim countries where the state is able to manipulate intellectuals to serve the regime ideology.

It seems obvious that the structure of the Central Institute for Islamic Research was determined to be semi-secular. As Masud pointed out[50], Fazlur Rahman, who was a graduate of Oxford University, and at the time of establishing the Institute was teaching at McGill University, Montreal, Canada, "gathered together a group

48   Ibid., p. 48.
49   Ibid., p. 102.
50   Muhammad Khalid Masud, "Islamic Research Institute", ISIM Newsletter 1/98, p. 43.

of scholars who represented not only various disciples but also different Islamic orientations. This group represented different Islamic schools of thought and ethnic and provincial diversity in Pakistan. In addition to their training in traditional Islamic learning, all had to have a degree in modern discipline, e.g. economy, sociology, political science etc. These scholars also had advanced degrees from renowned universities in the West. Several were sent to USA and Canada.

As the institute acted as an advisory think tank to assist in legislation work, it provided research material for the drafting of various laws. It assisted the Islamic Advisory Council, which would advise the National Assembly. Pakistan Family Laws, legislated in 1962, represented a liberal interpretation of the Qur'ân and Sunna.

The conservatives opposed these laws as they restricted polygamy and gave rights to women that traditional Islamic law did not allow. The institute found itself the target of hostile propaganda. Fazlur Rahman was called Abu'l Fazl, the notorious Vizir of the Mughal emperor Akbar who supposedly instituted a new religion.

Fazlur Rahman's book *Islam, a general introduction*, essentially written as a defense of Islam against Western critics, triggered controversy. A population with 25% literacy took to the streets protesting against a book that most of them could not and had not read. Political opposition to Ayyub took advantage of the situation. The `ulamâ` declared Rahman a heretic. Agitation started in Dacca, the constituency of Mawlana Ihtishamul Haq Thanawi who was leading this protest against Rahman and Ayyub Khân. Countrywide disturbances in 1969 caused Ayyub to resign. Rahman was forced to leave the country, and taught at the University of Chicago until his death in 1988.

12-Rethinking Qur'ân

We can briefly divide the orientation of modern exegesis of the Qur'ân into three basic trends, each of which essentially addresses one of the challenging questions mentioned above, i.e., science, reason and politics, that modernity brought to the mind of Muslims.

a- Islam and Science

It was the Indian Sayyid Ahmad Khân, whom we have already encountered, who looked at the question of science in his exegesis of the Qur'ân. As we have seen, both the criticism of hadîth and the consideration of the position of Sunna were meant to free the Qur'ânic exegesis from the heavy impact of tradition in order to facilitate the introduction of a rather more modern understanding of God's message. Criticizing classical Qur'ânic commentaries in terms of their sources and their subjects of interest, Ahmad Khân accepts only those parts of the commentaries dealing with the literary aspects of the Qur'ân. He points to anomalies in the interpretation of the Qur'ân and suggests that these are void of even general principles on which to base an understanding of the Holy Scripture.

Sayyed Ahmad Khân's major interest was to bring the meaning of the Qur'ân into harmony with the modern discoveries of the natural sciences. Natural scientific discoveries, he asserts, need to be taken into account while explaining the meanings of relevant parts of the Qur'ân, since they do not contain anything against the "law of nature".

Modern scientific discoveries, explains Sayyid Ahmad Khân, are the manifestations of God's promises in reality while the Qur'ân presents God's promises in words. On the basis of this argument he suggests that Scripture has to come to terms with the law of nature, which includes scientific discoveries. He therefore rejects miracles and many Qur'ânic descriptions, which he considers "supernatural" in their literal sense, and describes them as metaphors and indirect expressions of reality.[51]

He states that Qur'ânic words and expressions should not be understood exclusively in their direct literal meanings; the Holy Scripture often uses metaphors, allegories, and other indirect expressions. In order to give his claim an authentic traditional support, he explains how the classical `ulamâ' did not always accept literal meanings of many Qur'ânic words when such meanings contradict common sense or human intellect. The reason they recognized miracles,

51 See Sayyed Ahmad Khân, 'Tahrîr fî usûl al-Tafsîr' (writing on the principles of interpretation), in Tafsîr al-Qur'ân wa huwa al-hudâ wa'l-Furqân (Interpretation of the Qur'ân which is the Guide and the Proof) (Khuda Bakhsh Oriental Public Library: Patna, India, 2nd ed. 1995) vol. 1, pp. 1-20.

and, therefore, accepted supernatural Qur'ânic descriptions in their literal sense is because natural sciences were not sufficiently developed during those periods. But since very little is known about pre-Islamic Arabic literature, he concludes that it is possible that words and phrases have meanings other than those explained by lexicologists. It is therefore imperative also to apply other sources and to accept such meanings of the Qur'ân as are based on them, although these may be absent from dictionaries.[52]

Self-evidently the explicit concept of the Qur'ân as a Text, which has been the well established concept since its canonization, is uncritically accepted by Sayyid Ahmad Khân. That explains his admiration of that part of classical exegesis emphasizing the literary aspect. Although skeptical about the quantity of the knowledge available of pre-Islamic Culture, he methodologically emphasizes its importance. He concludes that the Qur'ân should, first and foremost, be understood, explained and interpreted by the Qur'ân itself i.e., by understanding its own internal structure. He considers such principle to be derived from the Holy Book.[53] The second methodological principle is that understanding the pre-Islamic Arabic literature is a pre-requisite to understanding the Qur'ân.

Methodologically speaking there is nothing new in Sayyid Ahmad Khân's presupposition. The difference between his interpretation and the classical commentaries, however, lays in the domain of meaning - the modern meaning - that considers science, especially natural science the new religion of secularism. Fascinated by the new world of science and discovery he had to find a way to integrate it into his holy scripture. I propose here that Sayyid Ahmad Khân's effort to open the meaning of the Qur'ân to accept scientific findings is the embryo of the later to be developed pair of seemingly opposite directions, namely the emphasis on the scientific inimitability of the Qur'ân[54], and that of islamization of knowledge and science.

52 Ibid, p. 15.
53 Ibid, pp. 2 and 13-15.
54 The scientific supremacy of the Qur'ân (al-i`jâz al-`ilmî), according to an article published in the weekly supplement of al-Ahrâm newspaper, October 27, 2000, p. 2, is not meant to convince the Arabs of the authenticity and divinity of the Qur'ân. For the Arabs, the writer says, it is enough to establish the Qur'â inimitability on its rhetorical eloquence; for the non-Arabs this explanation is neither enough nor acceptable. As for Western culture, science is the supreme mode of

b- Islam and Rationalism

Although Muhammad `Abdu was neither a theologian nor a philoso-
pher, he admired the philosophical and mystical knowledge of Jamâl
al-Dîn al-Afghânî (1839-1879). But while al-Afghânî was more of an
activist and provocative teacher[55] `Abdu gave up politics and con-
centrated his efforts in the arena of thought, especially after he was
exiled because of his participation in `Urabî's affair which ended with
the British occupation of Egypt in 1882. Influenced heavily by
Afghânî, who had brought to Egypt the idea of a new, modern interpretation of Islam, `Abdu adopted a synthesis of classical rationalism
and modern socio-political awareness. This made it possible for him

knowledge. The article is basically written in response to the criticism directed to
the notion of 'the scientific supremacy of the Qur'ân. It is claimed that connect-
ing the Qur'ân to scientific theory, which is changeable and subject to challenge
as human knowledge develops, does in fact cause damage to the divinity and the
eternity of the Qur'ân, the word of God. Defending the validity of al-i`ijâz
al-`ilmî the writer distinguishes between scientific facts and scientific theories
asserting that the Qur'ân's supremacy is built on the former not the later. If such
facts are explicitly or implicitly expressed in the Qur'ân, it represents the solid and
universal proof of its divinity. In this context the compatibility of Islam, specifi-
cally the Qur'ân, with modern science became one of the concerns of some non-
cleric Muslim intellectual. Reference can be made to publications including:
1 - Reveling the illuminating Qur'anic secrets Concerning the Celestial and
  Terrestrial Bodies, Animals, Plants and Metals (Kashf al-Asrâr 'l-Nawrâniyya
  'l-Qur'âniyya fimâ Yata`laqu b i'l-Ajrâm '-Samâwiyya wa 'l-Ardiyyah wa
  'l-Haywânat wa 'l-Nabâtât wa 'l-Jawâhir 'l-Ma`daniyya) by Mohammed b.
  Ahmed al-Iskandrani, Cairo 1297/1880;
2 - Explaining the Divine Secrets in Plants, Metals and the Specific Characteristics
  of Life (Tibyân al-Asrar '-Rabbâniyya fi 'l-Nabât wa 'l-Ma`âdin wa 'l-Khawâs 'l-
  Haywâniyya), Syria 1300/1883;
3 - Comparing Some of the Astrological Discovery with What is Mentioned in the
  Divine Texts (Muqâranat Ba`d Mabâhith al-Hay`a bi 'l-Wârid fi 'l Nussûs
  'Shar`iyyah) by `Abdullah Fikri, who was a Minister of Education in Egypt, Cairo
  1315/1897);
4 - The Precious Metals in the Interpretation of the Qur'ân (al-Jawâhir fi Tafsîr al-
  Qur'ân) by Tantawi al-Jawhari (d 1940), 26 vol., first printed unknown, 2ed.,
  Cairo 1350/1971. It is multi-volumes tafsîr in which the author tries his best to
  find everything related to modern science, modern technology, or even discoveries in the Qur'ân. Six verses, 5:27-32 for example, is dealt with in 25 pages including many headings starting with 'linguistic explanation, al-tafsîr al-lafzî' and end-
  ing with 'the iron save boxes' in the Qur'ân, al-khazâ'in al-hadîdiyah fi 'l-Qur'ân'.
  (cf. `Abd al-Majîd al-Sharafî, al-Islam wa 'l-Hadâtha (Islam and Modernity),
  Tunisia 1990, pp.69-76.
55 See, `Amârah, Muhammad (ed.), Al A`mâl al Kâmilah li Jamâl al-Dîn al-Afghânî
  ma`a Dirâsat Hayâtih wa Ââtharih (The Complete Collection of al-Afghânî's
  Writings, with a Study of his Life and his Writings), Cairo 1968, p. 29.

to re-examine the basic sources of Islamic knowledge, the Qur'ân and the Sunna as well as the structure of Islamic theology, thus, preparing the ground for what is known as the *islâh*, reformation, movement.

When he was appointed as the religious councellor, *muftî*, of Egypt in 1899[56], he addressed so many practical social and cultural issues that needed to be dealt with from an Islamic rational perspective. He set a program for the reform of Muslim higher education and for the reform of the administration of Muslim law. He tried to carry out these practical reforms, first, when he suggested reforms of education in general and of al-Azhar in particular in 1892, and, second, when he proposed so many plans for the reform of the legal system. `Abdu's efforts to introduce some reforms to al-Azhar was partly successful, but the resistance from the traditional `*ulamâ*' was so strong that he concentrated more on intellectual reformation.

His confidence in 'reason' is manifest in all his activities, although he considers that 'religion' provides the basis to protect 'reason' from erring. The question of Islam and modern knowledge, which was fundamental to `Abdu's writings, led him to re-examine Islamic heritage, pushing more to reopen the 'door of *ijtihâd*' in all aspects of social and intellectual life. As religion is an essential part of human existence, he argued that the only avenue through which to launch real reform was through a reform of Islamic thought.

He elaborated in his *Tafsîr al-Manâr* the concept of the Qur'ân as a 'text' by, first, emphasizing implicitly its literary structure, secondly, placing its style in expressing its message in the seventh century in accordance with intellectual level of the Arabs' mentality. Whatever seems irrational or contradictory to logic and science in the Qur'ân must, accordingly, be understood as reflecting the Arabs' vision of the world at that time. All verses referring to superstitions like witchcraft and the evil eye are to be explained as expressions of what the Arabs believed in. And literary figures of speech (like 'metaphor' and 'allegory') appear in *Tafsîr al-Manâr* as the basis of a rational explanation for all miraculous events and deeds mentioned in the Qur'ân. The verses which speak about sending the angels down from heaven to fight against the *kuffâr,* infidels, are thus

56   `Abdu, Muhammad, Al-A`mâl al-Kâmilah, op cited, vol. 5, pp. 105f.

explained by `Abdu as an expression of encouragement; they were meant to provide comfort to the believers, to help enable them to gain a victory.[57]

This was precisely the first explicit effort of the re-contextualization of the Qur'ân against the 7th century cultural background, a method that was developed by later Egyptian as well as Arab and Muslim intellectuals. This process of re-contextualization led `Abdu to de-mythologize the Qurânic narrative as well as to come close to a de-mystification of the Holy Text.

While Sayyid Ahmad Khân was trying to harmonize the Qur'ân with science, by way of creating equation between them - the equation between Divine 'promise in Action' and 'promise in words' - it was quite enough for `Abdu to place the Qur'ân in the seventh century context, thus excluding any attempt of comparison between the Qur'ân and science.

His most important contribution in this area was his insistence that the Qur'ân is not meant to be a book of history neither a book of science; it is a book of guidance. Consequently, any search of proof for any scientific theory is invalid. Qur'anic narratives, on the other hand, should not be taken as historical documents. Indeed, historical incidents mentioned in the Qur'anic narratives are presented in a literary and narrative style, to convey lessons of admonition and exhortation.[58] `Abdu was very clear about the difference between 'historiography' and the Qur'anic stories. Historiography is a scientific field of knowledge based on inquiry and critical investigation of available data (reports, testimonies, memories, and geographical or material evidences, for example). In contrast, the Qur'anic stories are intended to serve ethical, spiritual and religious purposes. They might be based on some historical incidents, but the purpose is not to provide knowledge about history. This explains why names of persons, places and dates are not mentioned in these stories. Even if the story is about a prophet, or about one of the enemies of a prophet (like Pharaoh), many details are omitted. `Abdu is clearly against the method of the classical exegetes, which attempted to clarify these *mubhamât* (unmentioned; non-explicit). He insisted that the impor-

57 ibid., vol. 5, pp. 506-11.
58 Ibid., vol. 5, p. 30f.

tance of the story does not depend on such knowledge; it depends rather on the lesson of 'admonition' that can be deduced from it.[59]

It is important here to emphasize the fact that `Abdu's intellectual liberal discourse presents the intellectual side of the modernizing project initiated by Muhammad `Ali (1760-1849) to establish a modern state in Egypt, a project that was carried out by his grandson Khedive Ismâ`îl (1863-1879), who explicitly wanted Egypt to be like any European state. The ideas of `Abdu were very influential during the twentieth century right across the entire Muslim World, thanks to journal of *al-Manâr* (1898-1936) established by Rashîd Rida (1865-1935), `Abdu's disciple and partner.

`Abdu's 'rational' oriented exegesis was not entirely free of the issue of modern science where it was implicit, neither was the 'science' oriented exegesis of Ahmad Khân free from rationalism. Like `Abdu, in his effort to free the field of Qurânic exegesis from tradition Ahmad Khân placed the principles of 'reason' and 'nature' as a substitute for the classical heavy dependence on quotations from tradition. His proposal is that the Qur'ân stands on its own, requiring only application of a dedicated and enlightened mind for its understanding. The principles of interpretation, according to Ahmad Khân, should not depend on hadîth or this will hazard the eternal and universal quality of the Qur'ân. For him, the great miracle of the Qur'ân is its universality which makes it possible for every generation to find in it the meaning relevant to its situation despite the constant increase in human knowledge. Hadîth-based interpretation tends to limit the meaning of the Qur'ân to a particular historical situation, thus, obscuring its universality.[60]

c- Islâm and Politics

Political concern is not absent from either the exegesis of `Abdu or Ahmad Khân. Neither is it appropriate to suggest that 'political' oriented exegesis was started by the Pakistani author, journalist, interpreter of the Qur'ân, ideologue and political activist Abu 'A`lâ

---

59 For a detailed account of Abdu's views concerning the Qur'anic narrative, see Tafsîr al-Manâr, Cairo 2ed reprint, vol. 1, pp. 19-21, 210-11, 215, 229-30, 233-4, 271; vol. 3, 47-8; vol. 4, pp. 7, 42, 92-3.
60 Rethinking Tradition, op, cited, p. 44.

Mawdûdî (1903-1979). But it was Abu 'l-A`lâ al-Mawdûdî who gave the political Islamic movement its qur'ânic ground that was copied by Sayyid Qutb. More than anyone else he shaped and influenced the further development of 'orthodox fundamentalism', also known as 'Islamism'.[61] The leaders of the Shi`ite revolution in Iran in 1979 gave as their main sources of inspiration for shaping an Islamic state the publications of their Egyptian Sunni 'Brethren' Hasan al-Bannâ and Sayyid Qutb, and the Pakistani Mawdûdî.

It goes without saying that it was in the Indian context under the British occupation, where the relationship between the Muslims and the Hindus started to deteriorate. Mawdûdî started his comprehensive study of the doctrine of jihâd in the mid-1920s, in response to Hindu accusations that Islam was spread by the sword, after a Muslim assassinated a non-Muslim leader. This work, which was first serialized then published under the title *al-jihâd fî 'l-Islâm*, presented the basic elements of his later thought. In 1932, and in the monthly journal *Tarjumân al-Qur'ân*, which was to be the main vehicle of his ideas for the rest of his life, Mawdûdî' started to formulate the ideology of political Islam. He set forth the objectives of his intellectual mission in the following lines:

> *The plan of action I had in mind was that I should first break the hold which Western culture and ideas had come to acquire over the Muslim intelligentsia, and to instill in them the fact that Islam has a code of life of its own, its own culture, its own political and economic systems and a philosophy and an educational system which are all superior to anything that Western civilization could offer. I wanted to rid them of the wrong notion that they needed to borrow from others in the matter of culture and civilisation.* [62]

---

61 Azia Ahmad, Islamic Modernism in India and Pakistan 1857-1965, Karachi, 1967, pp. 208-36. See also, Bassam Tibi, The Challenge of Fundamentalism; Political Islam and the New World Disorder, Updated Edition, Berkeley, 2002, p. 42; see also Tariq Ramadan, Aux sources de renouveau musulman, d'l-Afghani à Hassan al-Banna; un siècle de réfomisme islamique, Paris, 1998. All quoted by Jan Slomp, "The 'Political Equation' in Al-Jihâd Fî Al-Islâm of Abul A`la Mawdudi ", in A Faithful Presence, essays for Kenneth Cragg, edited by David Thomas and Clare Amos, London 2003, p. 239.

62 See F C R Robinson, 'Mawdûdî', in EI, vol., iv, pp. 872ff.

According to this ideology, where the West and Islam stand in dichotomy, the complex human societies are categorized in only two kinds, either 'Islamic' or '*Jâhilî*'. As long as the universe, according to the Mawdûdî's Islamic view, is an "organized state" and a "totalitarian system", in which all powers are vested in Allah, the only ruler, the state of Islam, or the Islamic State, should present the earthly manifestation of the cosmos.

If both 'Abdu and Ahmad Khân tried, in different way, to contextualize the Qur'ân in order to open up its meaning by way of allegorization and metaphorization, Mawdûdî extended the literal meaning of the Qur'ân to address the modern world. The verses of chapter 5:42-50, for example, - now well known as the verses of *hâkimiyya*, the absolute sovereignty of God - which addressed the people who rejected Islam during the time of the Prophet, are taken by Mawdûdî to be addressing the Muslims now; its meaning is not only to apply the rules prescribed by God but to establish a theocratic state.

Studying in detail Mawdûdî's book on jihad Slomp rightly comments on his hermeneutics as a hermeneutics that turns the decisions taken in certain historical moments into eternal divine law. For its importance I better quote it in its length.

> On the basis of Mawdudi's own arguments and examples the reader concludes, "that all statements on jihad in the Qur'ân, Hadith and early Islamic history were established in actual situation, and that they were formulated on the basis of decisions concerning for example slaves, spoils of war, prisoners, 'the hypocrites', traitors, treatment of enemies and minorities as part of a historical process. To declare the result of this process sacrosanct, as Maudidi does, reveals that the Achilles heel of this Islamism is its way of dealing with history. For all the events in the life of the Prophet and his Companions are given the same authority as revelation. Added to this, Mawdudi's interpretation of this 'revelation cum history' is presented as authoritative for Islam in all eras. [63]

---

63 Jan Slomp, "The 'Political Equation' in Al-Jihâd Fî Al-Islâm of Abul A'la Mawdudî", op cited, p. 255.

It could be concluded that Sayyid Ahmad Khân, `Abdu, and Mawdûdî have furnished the ground for Muslim intellectuals, throughout the twentieth century to open up the meaning of the Qur'ân, and consequently the meaning of Islam, to cope with modernity, in different ways. As illustrated Sayyid Ahmad was basically busy with the challenge of modern science; `Abdu was busy with the issue of 'rationality' in general; Mawdûdi was responding to the challenge of Western domination, and consequently the Westernization of the Muslim world. If Khân's approach is to be considered the embryo of the late '*al-i`jâz al-`ilmî*' as well as 'the islamization of science and knowledge' trend, `Abdu's approach was carried on in what has been known as the 'literary approach'. Mawdûdî's approach stands alone as the real source of the following political and ideological interpretation of the Qur'ân. Regardless of their differences in terms of methodology and conclusions, three of them followed the classical assumption that the Qur'ân is a text.

Now, once again the question is which meaning will prevail, togetherness or isolation? Related question to be raised is whether Muslims are ready to rethink the Qur'ân or not? Is it possible to consider the open options presented in the Qur'ânic discourse and reconsider the fixed meaning presented by the classical `*ulamâ*? In other words, how far is the reformation of Islamic thought going to develop? This duly brings the relationship of the West and the Muslim World into our discussion. How does this relationship affect the way Muslims 'rethink' their own tradition to modernize their lives without relinquishing their spiritual power, particularly in view of America's colonizing project? I am afraid the answer is not positive, especially with the new American colonization project. Both the new imperial and colonial American project and the building of ghettos in the Middle East are likely to support the most exclusive type of discourse in contemporary Islamic thought. We have to be alert and to join our efforts to fight against that by all possible means.

Conclusion

I have argued that the Qur'ân is a living phenomenon. A humanistic hermeneutics of the Qur'ân has to take seriously the living phenomenon and stop reducing the Qur'ân to be only a text. The Qur'ân was the outcome of dialoguing, debating, augmenting, accepting and rejecting. This horizontal, communicative and humanistic dimension is in the 'structure' of the Qur'ân, not outside it. The invitation to 'rethink the Qur'ân' flows from this communicative dimension. This invitation is of vital importance for Muslims in general, and for Muslims living in Europe in particular. I have argued not only for the continuation of this process of rethinking but for moving it further toward a constructive method for Muslims, wherever they are, to be actively engaged in formulating the 'meaning of life' in the world in which they live and further develop the spiritual and ethical dimension of their tradition.

But what will prevail: togetherness or isolation? Are Muslims ready to rethink the Qur'ân or not? Is it possible to consider the open options presented in the Quranic discourse and reconsider the fixed meaning presented by the classical `ulamâ'? In other words, how far is the reformation of Islamic thought going to develop? This question duly brings the relationship of the West and the Muslim World into the discussion. How does this relationship affect the way Muslims 'rethink' their own tradition to modernize their lives without relinquishing their spiritual power? I am afraid the answer is not positive, particularly in view of America's new colonizing policy. Both the new imperial and colonial project of the United States of America and the building of ghettos in the Middle East are likely to support the most exclusive and isolating type of discourse in contemporary Islamic thought. These colonial projects give the people no option but to adapt to the hermeneutics of Islam as an ideology of resistance; the hermeneutics of the Pakistân Maududi, which divides the world into two adversaries, echoed in Huntington's 'Clash of Civilizations'. So I conclude that we have to be alert and should join our efforts to fight both claims and their consequences by all possible democratic means.

COLOPHON

Rethinking the Qur'ân: Towards a Humanistic Hermeneutics
Nasr Abû Zayd

ISBN 90 6665 605 0
NUR 717

Layout and typesetting
Charley Klinkenberg, Amsterdam

Publisher
Dennis H. van Santen

For information on other SWP and
Humanistics University Press publications:
P.O. Box 257, 1000 AG Amsterdam
www.swpbook.com
swp@swpbook.com

Made in the USA
Middletown, DE
02 June 2019